BRIGHT NOTES

THE PLAYS OF EURIPIDES

Intelligent Education

Nashville, Tennessee

BRIGHT NOTES: The Plays of Euripides
www.BrightNotes.com

No part of this publication may be used or reproduced in any manner whatsoever without written permission, except in the case of brief quotations in critical articles and reviews. For permissions, contact Influence Publishers http://www.influencepublishers.com.

ISBN: 978-1-645424-46-8 (Paperback)
ISBN: 978-1-645424-47-5 (eBook)

Published in accordance with the U.S. Copyright Office Orphan Works and Mass Digitization report of the register of copyrights, June 2015.

Originally published by Monarch Press.
William Walter, 1964
2020 Edition published by Influence Publishers.

Interior design by Lapiz Digital Services. Cover Design by Thinkpen Designs.

Printed in the United States of America.

Library of Congress Cataloging-in-Publication Data forthcoming.
Names: Intelligent Education
Title: BRIGHT NOTES: The Plays of Euripides
Subject: STU004000 STUDY AIDS / Book Notes

CONTENTS

1)	Introduction to Euripides	1
2)	Alcestis	20
3)	Medea	26
4)	Hippolytus	40
5)	Heracleidae	53
6)	Andromache	58
7)	Hecuba	64
8)	Cyclops, A Satyr-Play	68
9)	Heracles	72
10)	Suppliants	77
11)	Ion	82
12)	Iphigenia in Tauris	87

13)	Helen	93
14)	Trojan Women	99
15)	Electra	111
16)	Orestes	124
17)	Phoenissae	130
18)	Bacchae	137
19)	Iphigenia in Aulis	152
20)	Rhesus	158
21)	Criticism	163
22)	Essay Questions and Answers	166
23)	Bibliography	177

INTRODUCTION TO EURIPIDES

BIRTH AND EARLY LIFE

The exact date of Euripides' birth has never been determined. Some say that he was born on the very day of the Athenian naval defeat of the Persians at Salamis in 480 B.C. Others say it was 484, and still others say it was 485. The precise date of Euripides' birth does not mean nearly so much as an understanding of the man, his work, and his era. And this will be a challenge to the reader, who will discover as he pursues a study of Euripides a most controversial and often misinterpreted figure.

The myths concerning his parentage and life make an amusing legend. It has been said that Euripides was the son of a woman who peddled vegetables. It has also been said that he grew to be a bookish, brooding recluse, a woman-hater, and a misfit who after two unsuccessful marriages moved to Macedonia. The end of his life in this barbarian country is said to have been mutilation by dogs who were put on him for his general subversiveness.

More reliable sources say that Euripides was born at Phlya, a village in central Attica, to a mother named Cleito who was of high birth. The immediate neighborhood of Euripides' early childhood was famous for its temples. In his youth, Euripides took part in the local religious festivals as both cup-bearer and fire-bearer. When he was four years old, the family was routed from its home because of the impending Persian attack. By the time he was eight, the ruins caused by the Persians' destruction were being rebuilt. When he reached the age of eighteen, he became officially known as an "Ephebus" or "Youth," which meant that he was provided with a spear and a shield and set to police duty along the forts of his city-state. Up to then his interests had been primarily in painting and athletics. In early manhood he came under the influence of such philosophers as Protagoras, Anaxagoras, Archelaus, Diogenes, and Socrates.

EARLY PLAYS

As previously stated (see Greek Tragic Drama) early Greek tragedies were part of the Great Festival of Dionysius for which three poets were selected to compete, and were given a Chorus subsidized by wealthy patrons. The poet's job was then to train the Chorus in the performance of the drama. At the end of each festival a body of five judges awarded first, second, and third prizes. Euripides became one of the selected poets in 455 B.C. and produced his first tragedy, the *Daughters of Pelias*, to which he later wrote the sequel, *Medea*. He did not win a first prize, however, until 442 B.C., but the name of his triumphant play is unknown. He continued to write plays, producing as many as four in one year, a feat which he accomplished in 438. These early plays showed Euripides' penchant for a moral investigation of taboos and the savage punishment of their violators. A certain note of discontent was beginning to be evident, and this was later to become one of Euripides' trademarks.

MIDDLE PERIOD

Medea (431 B.C.) was the next important play. It was poorly received by the judges, but later became recognized as one of the greatest of tragic dramas. *Hippolytus*, which followed three years later (428) won the first prize but it severely shocked the public at the time.

The Peloponnesian War, which began in 431 B.C. had a profound influence on Euripides' works during this middle period. The two most "patriotic" plays are *The Children of Heracles* or *The Heracleidae* (427) and *The Suppliants* (421), but patriotism can also be seen in certain aspects of *Medea*, *Andromache* (426), and *Heracles* (422). (*Cyclops*, written in 423, is the only satyr play surviving, and has no particular "message.") *Hecuba* (425) reveals the embittering experience of war which became a stamp on his later works. Euripides' patriotism was a matter of ideals, and, therefore, far stronger than mere acceptance of the propaganda he had received in his forty years of military service. (It was not unusual for men of ancient Greece to be on call for military duty as an obligation to the state, whatever his occupation.) The writing of *Heracles*, however, marks the end of Euripides' military service, as he was then sixty years old.

LATER PLAYS

The end of the Peloponnesian War was a defeat for Athens. That, combined with the decline of Periclean enlightenment through the corruption and embitterment caused by the long war, had a strong effect on the aging Euripides who had fought and written for his ideals. The plays which followed fall into three main groups. Those which are enigmatic, beautiful yet revealing Euripides' own clashing moods are *Ion* (417) and *The Trojan Women* (415). Next follow his light, fantastic or romantic works: *Iphigenia in Tauris* (414) and *Helen* (412). Then there are the ruthless tragedies showing Euripides' profound bitterness and growing despair. These are *Phoenissae* (409), *Electra* (413), and *Orestes* (408). The later plays show the psychological **realism** and moral inquiry for which the earlier *Hippolytus* is so famous. Euripides, never especially popular because of his connections with the god-denying Sophists, had become the butt of satiric plays, a reputed misogynist because of the women depicted in his plays, and an overt critic of Athenian politics and involvement in the war. In short, the Athenians bore grudges and grievances against him which promoted his already reclusive tendencies. His two marriages had not been happy ones.

EXILE AND DEATH

In 408 Euripides suddenly left Athens. He went first to Magnesia but did not stay there long. Archelaus, the king of Macedon, renewed an invitation to Euripides to join the other Greek intellectuals and artists at the Macedonian court. Although Macedonia was not quite as civilized and cultivated as Athens, it offered Euripides the comfort and ease of royal patronage in a kingdom that was becoming more and more powerful. At most, Euripides lived eighteen months in Macedon. The actual facts of his death are not certain. It has long been rumored that he was accidentally mutilated by some of the king's Molossian hunting dogs who overtook him sitting in a wood.

After his death, three plays were found. The two most important of these are the *Iphigenia in Aulis* and the *Bacchae*, both of which were completed by his third son, the young Euripides.

GREECE IN THE FIFTH CENTURY B.C.

Early History

General Comments

Very little is known about the origin of Greek civilization. From the mainland, small waves of successive migrations took place moving outward into the island of the Aegean Sea, finally stopping at the coast of Asia Minor. The name given to this mixed populace of invaders and conquered peoples was Hellenes. At no time were they a homogeneous nation, although they were related by certain common cultural traits which differentiated them from "barbarians" or non-Hellenes of the Asian mainland. Divided either by mountains or sea from its neighbor, each community was a separate political unit which came to be known as a city-state. The earliest literary record of the Greeks is the work of Homer whose *Iliad* and *Odyssey*, composed around 850 B.C. refer to events dating back three hundred years.

Homeric Greece (1000-800 B.C.)

Introduction

The period described in Homer's works was an aristocratic one. The king, or "basileus" was not the absolute ruler, although he was the military, religious, and judicial officer. The king consulted on affairs of state with numerous lesser chiefs who were drawn from heads of great families. Often these consultations were held in the form of public debate. The commoners did not vote but could make their sentiments known by disapproving silence or shouts of approbation. Life was simple and primitive -mainly agricultural - until about the end of the ninth century when economical development began with maritime commerce. Industrial progress was influenced largely by the middle eastern countries who served as models for the Hellenes in matters of economics. The coinage of money began in the eighth century as the textile, leather, ceramic, and wood industries flourished along with a large export trade in olives and wines. A great period of colonization of the outer islands began at the end of the eighth century and lasted for two hundred years. This phenomenon was the result of increasing ranks of landless peasants whose holdings had been diminished by the encroachment of large estates and whose economic deprivation often placed them in bondage. To alleviate these conditions and to prevent the danger of a growing indentured or mendicant population, colonies were founded.

Political Development

The great landowners, or nobles, gradually assumed more and more political power. This concentration of power in the hands of a few changed the structure of government from monarchy to oligarchy. The citizenry responded to this development with growing demands for a voice in the government. The leaders of the citizens' groups who offered to depose ruling families in exchange for popular support were called "tyrants" after having seized power. Their position was totally dependent upon the concessions they made to the people. Thus the form of government changed from oligarchy to "tyranny," a word which had not the ugly **connotations** of today. Tyranny paved the way for democracy because it was based on a concept of concession to the populace, and tyrants who ignored their obligations were fairly easily deposed.

The Archaic Period (800-500 B.C.)

Athens And Sparta

Two cities that played a major role in the development of Greek civilization during the Archaic Period were Athens and Sparta. By the seventh century Sparta had become a conservative military state, governed by an aristocracy comprised of two kings who had nominal power and five magistrates, as well as a Council of Elders who shared the real power with the magistrates. Spartan culture was devoted to a rigid code of discipline and was contemptuous of intellectual aesthetic pursuits. Athens, on the other hand, had passed through every phase of government from monarchy to democracy by the end of the sixth century. The Athenians were progressive, individualistic, and devoted to intellectual and aesthetic culture, particularly philosophy, literature, and art. The majority of political progress was accomplished by three tyrants: Solon, who instituted fundamental reforms in citizenship privileges; Pisistratus, whose land reform transferred property from the nobility to the peasants; and Cleisthenes, whose political reforms laid the foundations for Athenian democracy. Eventually, however, Athenian democracy became an exclusive affair, bestowing the privileges of citizenship only on those with Athenian ancestry.

The Persian And Peloponnesian Wars

The rise of the Persian Empire during the sixth century (B.C.) posed a threat to the Greek city-states whose main concern heretofore had been individual development and quarrels among themselves. Before the end of the sixth century the Persian Empire had conquered the Ionian Greek cities on the coast of Asia Minor. In 499 Athens sent aid to the rebellious Greek cities, but the revolt was crushed, and the Persian king, Darius, became sufficiently aware of the Greeks' independent spirit to make him determined to conquer all the Aegean islands and the cities on the Greek mainland. The next Persian attack was directed mainly against Athens in 490. Not waiting for aid from Sparta which was on the way, the Athenians, with an army half the size of the Persians' attacked with such fury that the battle of Marathon became a decisive victory for the Greeks and stayed the Persians for ten years. In 480, under Darius' son, Xerxes, the Persians attacked again. By this time Athens and other Greek cities had formed an allied army and navy under Spartan leadership. The Athenian navy defeated the Persian fleet in the Straits of Salamis while the combined Greek armies defeated the Persians at Plataea.

After the Persian war, Athens became the leader of the Greek cities in a maritime alliance to patrol and defend Greek interests in the Aegean against the Persians. This alliance was known as the Council of Delos, where its headquarters were located. Within twenty-five years Athens dominated the confederation, and in 454 the treasury was moved from Delos to Athens. Those cities who resented Athenian domination attempted to withdraw but were retained in the confederacy by force. In addition, Athens interfered in the internal affairs of these cities, attempting to promote democratic governments which would be subservient to Athenian policies. Sparta, at the head of a rival confederacy of Peloponnesian cities, grew more antagonistic to Athenian machinations. The inevitable war between Athens and Sparta and their respective allies which lasted from 431 to 404 B.C. became known as the Peloponnesian War. The eventual result was the surrender of the Athenians and the break-up of her empire. Sparta then engaged in a fourteen-year war with Persia. The Greeks were eventually conquered by Macedonia.

The Golden Age

The Glory That Was Greece

The period with which we are mainly concerned is known as the "Golden Age" and covers the greater part of the fifth and fourth centuries, beginning before the Persian War and lasting beyond the Macedonian conquest. In these years Athens and other Greek cities produced their finest works of classical art and made the most memorable progress in philosophy, literature, and science. In general it may be said that the cultural goal of the Golden Age was a combination of clarity, simplicity, and proportion, motivated by high seriousness and dedicated to giving eternal validity to the understanding of man and nature.

From about 461 to 430 B.C. Athenian culture reached its peak of development. This period is called the Age of Pericles, named for the brilliant statesman under whose guidance Athens flourished. Under his administration, the buildings on the Acropolis in Athens which had been demolished by the Persians were reconstructed. Religious fervor and civic patriotism combined to make the Greek temples and civic buildings supreme feats of architecture. Sculpture and painting of equal greatness, depicting mostly human figures, recreated daily life, religion, and myth. Lyric poetry was another achievement of this period, remembered now more for its perfection of form than its content. The greatest poetry, combined with the most profound contemplation of human life, was the work of the dramatists.

Myth And Religion

The religion of the Greeks was polytheistic (the worship of multiple gods). The many gods of the Greeks were anthropomorphic (resembling man in appearance and character), superhuman in their powers, but very much like humans in their motivations and behavior. Although their characters and functions overlapped somewhat, the more important gods were easily distinguished. The worship of the gods was not subject to a systematized theology; indeed, the rituals of worship varied widely. The adventures of the gods and their relationships with each other and with mortals formed a rich body of mythology. Myth, in turn, became identified with spiritual and moral tenets, and functioned often to explain to the Greeks the phenomena of their physical world. Eventually, Greek drama came to have a civic and religious function, and in keeping with the function of the drama, myth was the suitable source for its plot and substance.

Rationality

One of the chief traits of the Greeks was their propensity for a rational explanation of things. Whether this explanation was based on myth or on human experience, it was nevertheless an essential element of Greek life. As faith in the gods of Homeric mythology gradually ceased to satisfy fundamental questions regarding the nature of man's surroundings, many new answers were drawn from philosophical and scientific speculation. Such hypotheses as Empedocles' (490-430 B.C.) that the world was composed of four elements-earth, air, fire, and water-or Hippocrates' theory that the body was made up of four elements-blood, phlegm, bile, and black bile-lasted for two thousand years as the basis of European scientific thought. Among the other achievements of the rational Greek mind was the triumph of philosophy. The great philosophers of the fifth and fourth centuries, Socrates, Plato, and Aristotle, attempted to explain the nature of the universe and to solve the moral and ethical problems of men. As a means of achieving the most perfect form of individual and social life, the philosophers believed that these problems could be solved by clear, logical, rational thought.

GREEK TRAGIC DRAM

Origins

Although as obscure as the origins of the Greeks themselves, the beginnings of Greek drama have been traced to the last half of the sixth century (B.C.) during the reign of the tyrant Pisistratus. In the process of building Athens into a city of great importance, he reorganized certain national festivals-among them the Festival of Dionysius (god of the vine and fertility, around whom certain mystery cults were formed). Various forms of drama, such as dramatic dances, character-mimes, ritual performances and, in particular, the dithyrambic hymn and dance to Dionysius were already a part of Greek culture. The dithyrambic hymn, a type of choral poem, was gradually becoming more dramatic, and according to Aristotle, was the basis of what evolved as the Greek drama. In this early dramatic form, the Leader of the Chorus detached himself and carried on a lyrical dialogue with the rest of the Chorus whose function was to narrate the stories of gods and heroes. A very early creator of this form of drama was a man named Thespis of whom virtually nothing is known. We do know, however, that Pisistratus incorporated Thespis' form into his new festival. The early association of the drama with a religious festival was never lost, and the theater never became a commercial enterprise. Instead, an official, chosen by lot, selected the plays to be presented. The state supplied the actors and selected wealthy citizens to support the preparations of the Choruses.

New Forms

Early in the fifth century, Aeschylus (525-456 B.C.) introduced a second actor into the performance and used dialogue as the means of unfolding his story. Thus emerged the dramatic form which we recognize today. Sophocles (496-406 B.C.), a younger contemporary and rival of Aeschylus, refined the technique of the elder dramatist by an increased number of actors, a sharper delineation of character, and a concentration on one single tragic issue. Both Aeschylus and Sophocles wrote with objectivity, always withholding personal views from their plays. Euripides (c. 480-407 B.C.), however, did not refrain from expressing his personal opinions via the characters in his tragedies. The characters of Euripides are generally known for their realistic portrayal, in contrast to the idealistic characterizations of Aeschylus and Sophocles, who depended largely on the Chorus to reveal the traits of their characters. Euripides also minimized the role of the Chorus and introduced the romantic or irrational element into his plays as a means of revealing psychological insight.

Subject Matter

The stories dramatized for tragedy were usually taken from mythology. [Comedy, which developed later, was drawn from the events of everyday life, for it was meant to be strictly a form of amusement. Hence, current doctrines and well-known personages were held up to **satire** and ridicule in the comedies. The only works of Greek comedy which remain are those of Aristophanes (448-388 B.C.).] His plots, although raucous, fantastic, and witty, contain much underlying **realism** in their **satire** on contemporary life.) However, the use of legends from traditional mythology as the sources of tragedy did not eliminate invention, for there were often numerous versions of individual myths. In any case, the dramatist would be obliged to focus his material, supply the details of motivation, and create a series of actions relevant to his **theme**. Sometimes even well-known legends were simply changed, especially by Euripides. The kind of suspense in most of these tragedies, then, involves not so much a curiosity as to what will happen as to how it will happen.

A special effect of Greek drama, frequently lost on the modern reader, is that of dramatic **irony**. This is produced when the audience knows what is going to happen to a character who speaks in ignorance of his future. A double meaning is thus given to what he says.

Perhaps the greatest quality of tragedy attributable to the use of mythological material is seriousness and dignity. Persons and events associated with religion, known individually to the gods-some with divine parents-and with a quasi-historical verisimilitude, give a kind of exalted reality to tragedy. Perhaps the closest equivalent in the Hebrew-Christian tradition is the group of legends in the Old Testament.

The Theater

Both tragedies and comedies were presented in the open-air theater (theatron or koilon), semi-circular in shape. Tiers of seats ranged upward from the lowest level, frequently taking advantage of sloping ground to form a natural amphitheater. The size of the theaters attests the popularity of drama: the Theater of Dionysus in Athens could seat 17,000.

At the lowest level was a flat round area called the orchestra, or dancing place. In its center was an altar to Dionysus which was also used as a stage property in many plays. Facing the altar, in the first row center, sat the priest of Dionysus. Forming the flat end of the semi-circle was the skene, or scene building. It was a wooden or stone structure which represented the front of a house, palace, or temple, and most of the action took place on a low platform at its base (the proskenion). The three doors of the skene were used for actors' entrances as required, although most entrances, including those of the Chorus, would be made from either side, through the parodoi. The orchestra was used for the choral dances and for whatever action might require the actors to move forward.

The top of the skene was also used for scenes set on the roof of a building. From there descended the **deus ex machina**, the "god from the machine" used so frequently by Euripides. Since gods would be expected to descend from above, a mechanical contrivance was used to lower them to the acting area. The device, of course, is less important than the dramatic use made of it. Since the material of the plays was nearly always mythological in origin, the appearance of gods was to be expected. It will be noted in reading the plays, however, that the gods as dramatized are rarely performers of magic who twist the action of the mortal characters about regardless of realistic possibilities. Usually, the

deus ex machina gives divine approval to some action which has already been worked out, or may foretell the future, thus concluding the story or even relating it to topical events. (*Rhesus* has an interesting exception.)

Another important stage device was the eccyclema, a platform which could be rolled out to reveal a tableau representing events which had taken place off stage. The most frequent use of the eccyclema in tragedy is for those scenes in which the stage directions in modern translations read: "The palace doors are thrown open to reveal the bodies of . . . ." Over or near the tableau, the actor who committed the murder would then deliver his speech, usually one of justification.

Performances were given twice a year: in January/February for the Lenaea, or festival of the winepress, and in March/April for the Festival of Dionysus called the Greater or City Dionysia. In fifth-century Athens, until the Peloponnesian War began, the latter festival ran for six consecutive days.

In addition to being religious festivals, the dramatic presentations were contests in which first, second, and third prizes were awarded. Each tragic dramatist was required to submit a tetralogy (a group of four plays). Three were tragedies and the fourth a lighter piece. The three plays might or might not be related to one another. Although "trilogy" means simply a group of three, it is frequently used to describe, in Greek tragedy, three plays about the same story, or group of events. Each individual play, however, would be a separate dramatic entity. Only one trilogy has survived complete. Aeschylus' *Oresteia*:

The fourth play of a tetralogy was usually a satyr-play, deriving its name from its Chorus, which always consisted of Satyrs. These are mythological creatures, represented as men with pointed ears, short horns, and goat legs. They were attendants of Dionysus, the god of fertility and wine. Fond of riotous living and lechery, they took frank and indecent pleasure in drinking and love-making. They were usually accompanied by Silenus, an aged Satyr. This aspect of the Chorus has an obvious connection with the god in whose honor the drama festivals were held, and the plays offered a light diversion after several hours of often very serious theater. The only complete satyr-play to survive is Euripides' *Cyclops*.

All plays were presented during the day, and only very rarely, therefore, does the action call for a night scene. The actors themselves were always men, and always wore painted masks, perhaps so everyone could see the dominant emotion of the character being presented. The number of speaking actors on the stage at one time did not exceed three. Any single actor could change mask and costume off stage and re-enter as a different character. A certain larger-than-life appearance was given the actor by the use of the cothurnus, the high-soled tragic boot. Masks and costumes were apparently conventional for character-types most frequently represented, and the audience would guess their identity immediately.

From a modern viewpoint, most aspects of the Greek theater seem confining, and, in fact, relatively little experimentation which would involve changing the physical appearance of the theater occurred. The fourth actor, though the need for him became more apparent, never appeared in tragedy; the Chorus, though its role became smaller, never disappeared. The amazing thing is the variety and dramatic effects produced within the severe limits of the theater conventions.

STRUCTURE OF TRAGEDY

The plots of Greek tragedies cannot be reduced to a single type. Certain formal divisions of each play are, however, almost invariable and are described below:

Prologue

This introductory section recounts background needed for understanding the action of the play. It is usually expository rather than dramatic, and indicates the starting point of subsequent action.

Parados

The entrance of the Chorus, chanting or singing. The verses usually contain further expositional background and set the emotional tone of the play.

Episodes And Stasimon

The action begins with the first **episode**, which follows the parados. Although the number of **episodes** in plays varies, it apparently was eventually fixed at five-the origin of the later **convention** of five acts. **Episodes** are separated by complete choral odes called stasima. The Chorus, or its leader, sometimes speaks during an **episode**, and a character sometimes speaks during, or is part of, a stasimon.

Exodos

The section after the last stasimon. It contains the final action of the play-usually not the "reversal" or climax-and a choral comment. Two features frequently appearing in the exodos are the messenger speech (which may also occur earlier in the play) and the deus ex machina.

Chorus

There is always a Chorus in Greek tragedy; indeed, tragedy itself originated with choral songs to which actors were added. Almost constantly present, the Chorus fulfills a number of functions. Its members not only sing, but dance and play musical instruments. A frequent function of the Chorus or of its leader (coryphaeus) is to question new characters coming on stage as to their origin and purpose. They have been called the ideal audience, reacting to the action as the poet would most desire. In fact, many people who had at one time or another performed in the Chorus were probably in the audience-accounting for some of the theatrical sophistication of Athenian audiences.

By their responses to the action, the Chorus modulates the atmosphere and tone. Usually representing what might be called "typical Athenian citizens," their reactions tend to be conservative, but not submissive. Passive, and without any particular involvement in the action's outcome in most plays, some extreme variations are noteworthy. In Aeschylus' *The Suppliants*, they are the **protagonist**. In Euripides' *Bacchae*, they are partisans of Dionysus. And in Euripides' *Helen,* they are little more than the performers of decorative interludes.

Since the stage had no curtains, and the plays no act divisions, the choral odes represented the passage of time-a flexible interval extending from a few minutes to several days or weeks. Although the major divisions of the plays are not indicated in most English translations, the divisions of choral odes are. The Chorus is usually divided into two parts, giving a symmetrical visual effect on stage. The first lyric they sing is called the strophe ("movement") and the second, metrically equivalent, the antistrophe ("counter-movement"). The afterpiece, marking the end of a stasimon, is called the epode. A lyric exchange of lamentation between the Chorus and an actor is called a kommos.

As tragedy developed, the role of the Chorus lessened. In Aeschylus' *The Suppliants* half the play is choral; in many of Euripides' less than a quarter. In late tragedy the constant presence of the Chorus became an obvious hindrance to the poet; even the conventional vow of secrecy became contrived. The day of its disappearance was not far off.

THE PLAYS OF EURIPIDES

ALCESTIS

....

BACKGROUND

Alcestis was presented as the fourth play of a tetralogy, instead of the usual satyr-play; this accounts for the play's comic elements and its happy ending.

Apollo's son, Asclepius, was killed by Zeus. Apollo avenged the death by killing the Cyclopes, one-eyed giants who supplied Zeus with lightning. Zeus punished Apollo by sentencing him to serve as slave to a human being, Admetus. Admetus was always kind to his slaves, and when the Fates decreed his early death, Apollo persuaded them to spare him if a substitute could be found. After his parents and friends had refused to die for Admetus, his wife, Alcestis, offered to make the sacrifice. When the play begins she is on her death bed.

CHARACTERS

Apollo: God sentenced to serve in household of King Admetus as a slave.

Death

Chorus: Old men.

Alcestis: Wife of Admetus, who offers to die in his place.

Admetus: King of Thessaly, fated to die prematurely.

Eumelus: Son of Admetus and Alcestis.

Heracles: Son of Zeus by a mortal, Alcmene. Famous for great strength and his "twelve labors."

Pheres: Father of Admetus.

Woman Servant

Man Servant

SETTING

In front of the palace of King Admetus, in Thessaly, the largest division of Greece; on the Aegean Sea, north of the Peloponnesus.

The play opens with a prologue in which Apollo tells why he is serving as a slave, and why Alcestis is dying (see "Background" above). Although fond of Admetus, Apollo is leaving the palace because of the imminence of death, which was regarded as polluting to the gods. Death enters to claim Alcestis. Apollo argues with him that he should wait till she is old, but Death regards the young as the greatest prize. Apollo prophesies that Alcestis will be taken from Death by force.

The Chorus of old men, knowing Alcestis' death to be near, enter with lamentations. A servant woman extolls Alcestis as a wife so perfect she is willing to die for her husband. While the Chorus pray to Zeus to spare Alcestis, she emerges from the palace, supported by Admetus and accompanied by their two children. In a frenzy of fear, Alcestis says she sees Charon, ferryman of the dead, dragging her to Hades. She reminds Admetus that, although he was his parents' only child, they refused to die for him. Therefore, in return for her sacrifice, Alcestis asks him never to remarry and set a stepmother over her children. Admetus, after telling how he hates his parents, promises. He also swears to have no more banquets and to revere an image he will make of his wife. Overcome by emotion, he begs that he may die with her. Alcestis dies, and her son Eumelus chants a lament. Admetus orders the country into strict mourning for a year.

Comment

Admetus' grief is genuine in this scene and helps to mitigate his selfishness in allowing his wife to die for him. Alcestis' request that he not remarry is motivated by concern for her children and not by jealousy of a successor: treatment of stepchildren, especially in royal households, was notorious.

The Chorus praise Alcestis as the perfect wife, predicting that many poets will praise her devotion.

Heracles enters, wearing the traditional lion-skin over his shoulders and carrying a large club. He is on his way to perform one of his famous labors-that of capturing the mares of King Diomedes of Thrace.

Comment

This was the eighth labor of twelve. The mares fed on human flesh. Heracles fed them their master, after which they became tame.

Admetus comes out in mourning and greets Heracles, who inquires the cause for his grief. Admetus, famous for his hospitality, lets him think the mourning is for a distant relative; Heracles would leave if he knew the truth. When Heracles has gone to the guest quarters, the Chorus criticize Admetus for taking a guest while in mourning for his wife; he tells them it would have been an insult to have let him go somewhere else. The Chorus sing a song of praise to Admetus' hospitality.

The funeral procession of Alcestis enters. Pheres, Admetus' father, praises Alcestis for having saved the life of his only son. Admetus furiously attacks Pheres for having refused to die for him, arguing that his father, having lived out his days, should have been willing. Pheres replies that no one has to die for another; life is as sweet for him as for his son. If anyone is to be blamed, he says, it is Admetus himself, who shirked his fate. The two men fiercely vituperate one another while the Chorus try to quiet them. Before going out, Pheres says Admetus has murdered Alcestis and that her brother will seek revenge. Admetus curses both his parents and forbids them to ever enter his house. The funeral procession passes off the stage.

Comment

The quarrel with Pheres forces Admetus to realize the way others will see him for allowing Alcestis' sacrifice; this may account for his changed attitude later in the play. The quarrel can also be read as symbolic of the conflict between the parental and marital loyalties of an individual.

A servant comes out of the palace and complains to the Chorus of Heracles' rude behavior; not only is he making demands rather than waiting to be served, but he is getting drunk. Heracles comes boisterously after the servant to accuse him of being sullen and impolite. The servant tells him that it was Alcestis who died. Completely sobered by the news, Heracles is so impressed by Admetus' hospitality that he resolves to attack Death near Alcestis' tomb and bring her back.

Comment

The basic comic situation in this play lies in the incongruity between the house of mourning and the brawling and drunken behavior of Heracles. The comedy is transformed into fine **irony** when Heracles, impressed by the extent of Admetus' hospitality, returns Alcestis.

The grief-stricken Admetus returns from the funeral. He now knows what misery living without Alcestis will entail; and, though unimaginative, he sees that he will be thought of as a coward who allowed his wife to die for him.

The Chorus say that Fate is a higher deity than Zeus; they try to console Admetus by saying that his wife was the noblest of women, and that her tomb will become a shrine.

Heracles enters with a veiled woman and, saying he must leave, asks Admetus to keep her until he returns. Admetus refuses, saying it would not be proper for him to harbor a young woman; besides she reminds him of Alcestis, and the sight of her would increase his grief. Heracles suggests that Admetus should take another wife; Admetus is horrified. However, out of respect for Heracles, he agrees to keep the veiled woman a short time. When Heracles persuades him to take one of the woman's hands in his right hand, she is revealed to be Alcestis. The only condition put upon her restoration is that she will not speak for three days, when she will be purified from her contact with death. Heracles leaves, Admetus declares a general celebration, and the Chorus say that the ways of the gods are indeed unpredictable.

THE PLAYS OF EURIPIDES

MEDEA

BACKGROUND

Medea was produced in Athens during the first year of the Peloponnesian War. Rivalry between Athens and Corinth ran high, and the appearance of Medea, who hated Corinth, would have special appeal for Athenians. The story had various versions; Euripides was possibly the first to represent Medea as the slayer of her children. One of the most celebrated of Greek tragedies, *Medea* has had enormous influence on subsequent literature and art.

A group of Greek heroes, known as the Argonauts ("sailors of the Argo"), sailed to Colchis under the command of Jason, the son of Aeson, in search of the Golden Fleece. To pass into the Black Sea Jason had to have the ship rowed quickly through the Clashing Rocks (Symplegades) (ll. 1-6). Once in Colchis, Aeetes, the king of the Colchians, compelled Jason to yoke and plow a field with a pair of fire-snorting bulls; then he had to overcome the vigilant serpent that guarded the Golden Fleece in its coils. Jason was able to accomplish these acts only with the aid of Medea, a sorceress and daughter of Aeetes (ll. 476-482), who had fallen in love with him. The pair left Colchis for Iolcus, but were pursued by Aeetes, whom Medea delayed by killing her brother and strewing his limbs on the sea behind her. The ship returned to Iolcus (ll. 166f., 1334f., 209-212, 7, 484). There Pelias, Jason's uncle, had killed Jason's father and usurped the throne. To get revenge, Medea convinced Pelias' daughters that by cutting their father in pieces and boiling him, they would restore his youth. Pelias' son then drove Jason and Medea into exile, and they fled with their two sons to Corinth (11. 486f., 9-11). Jason later deserted Medea to marry the daughter of Creon, king of Corinth (ll. 10-19). It is at this point that Euripides' play takes up.

CHARACTERS

Nurse: Of Medea, now her confidential handmaiden.

Tutor: Cares for Medea's children.

Medea: Wife of Jason, who has deserted her for the daughter of King Creon.

Chorus: Women of Corinth.

Creon: King of Corinth.

Jason: Husband of Medea, now son-in-law to king Creon.

Aegeus: King of Athens, offers refuge to Medea.

Messenger: Brings news from the palace of Creon.

Two Children: Sons of Jason and Medea.

SETTING

In front of Medea's house in Corinth, about fifty miles west of Athens.

Prologue (1-130)

The Nurse comes out of the house and laments that Jason and the Argonauts ever set out in quest of the golden fleece-then Medea would never have fallen in love with Jason, never have tricked the daughters of Pelias into slaying their father, and never have come to live in Corinth, where Jason has betrayed her and their children for King Creon's daughter. Medea is not to blame, for her desire has always been to please her husband. She is unable to eat and even hates the sight of her children. The Nurse knows Medea's moods and is afraid she will kill Jason and Creon. The Tutor comes in with the two children and asks the Nurse why she has left Medea alone. Her grief, the Nurse replies, was unbearable, and she had to come outside and proclaim it aloud to the heavens.

Comment

Euripides is always at great pains to motivate the exists and entrances of his characters, and here even explains the presence of the Nurse in what could have been left as the usual expository prologue of Greek tragedy.

In addition to giving us basic information about the setting and the characters of the play (remember that there were no playbills in antiquity), the prologue, told by someone very close to Medea, accomplishes two additional points: a) it tells us how much Medea is suffering from Jason's betrayal of her love, so that our sympathies are, from the very first, with Medea; and b) since the worst retribution that the Nurse imagines Medea will take is the murder of Jason and Creon, it makes Medea's actual vengeance, the slaughter of her own children, appear all the more strange and barbaric.

The Tutor says that even worse misfortunes are in store for Medea: Creon plans to banish her and her two children. The Nurse finds it shocking that Jason will permit such treatment of his sons. She warns the Tutor to keep the children away from their mother because she is in a dangerous mood.

Comment

Euripides could easily have had the Nurse know of this when she recited the prologue. But by holding back this last piece of information (told, for additional effect, in front of the children) it appears as suffering being added to suffering, thus increasing our sympathy for Medea.

From inside the house comes Medea's voice, cursing Jason and the children. That Medea should make the children suffer for their father's crime, the Nurse attributes to the nature of people in high places; unaccustomed to obedience and the suffering it imposes, they do not know how to suffer-when fortune turns against them, they strike back in every way they can. She recommends moderation as the only way to avoid misfortune.

Comment

As in much of Greek tragedy, the sin of excess (hubris) is here felt to be the cause of misfortune. The Chorus, and other characters who extol the virtues of moderation, usually belong to a class lower, poorer, or otherwise more unfortunate than those being criticized. The Nurse's consciousness of class as a factor controlling moral standards presents the case in unusually explicit form.

Parodos (131-213)

The Chorus of Corinthian women enter, having heard the lamentations of Medea. They are curious to know what misfortune has befallen a house they have come to love.

Comment

To get sympathy for Medea, usually represented as a monster, Euripides directs the audience's attention to Jason's despicable character, has the Nurse sympathize with her, and has the women of a town where she is a foreigner express their fondness for her.

Medea, offstage, cries out to Artemis and Themis, asking first for her own death and then for the death of Jason and his bride. The Chorus ask the Nurse to bring her outside, hoping they can console her. The Nurse offers to try, but sardonically adds that mankind has foolishly invented music and songs for banquets, where they are not needed, but can find no music to allay grief.

Comment

It is somewhat ironic that Medea calls upon Themis, the personification of precedent upon which all laws are based, and Aphrodite, the goddess of love, for whose sake Medea violated so harshly the spirit of Themis. But then it is typical of people (and perhaps of women more than men) when wronged to irrationally forget the wrongs that they themselves have committed.

First Episode (214-409)

Medea, trying to appear self possessed, emerges from the house. She proposes to justify herself, knowing the reputation people get by remaining silent. She appeals to the Chorus as women, who know the difficulties of woman's lot: they must buy a husband at great price and may find they have set a tyrant over themselves; they cannot obtain divorces; they must adjust to new ways of living, having almost to be prophets to guess what will please husbands; they have to give birth to children, something far more painful than the wars men complain about. Her own situation is doubly hard as a foreigner with no family to help her. From the Chorus she asks one boon, silence, should she find some plan to avenge herself with.

Comment

With the Chorus always on stage where they could hear crucial plans they might tell others, it became a **convention** of Greek tragedy to enjoin them to silence. In this play, Euripides, not content to rely on **convention**, motivates the Chorus' promise of silence with Medea's powerful rhetoric.

The low political status of foreign-born brides that Medea complains of is exactly that which prevailed in Athens at the time of the production of *Medea,* so that, in a certain sense, the play can be considered as a political commentary by Euripides.

Creon, King of Corinth, enters and tells Medea that she and her children have been banished from the city. He knows her reputation as a sorceress and has heard of her threats; he fears especially for his daughter. Medea pleads for a twenty-four-hour delay so she can find some place to go and arrange some support for her children. Creon reluctantly grants the request, but acknowledges that he is probably making a mistake. After he leaves, Medea tells the Chorus that she fawned on him only to gain enough time to effect her revenge. She vows to kill Jason, Creon, and his daughter. She ponders various methods and her means of escape afterwards. Should worst come to worst, she vows to kill them with a sword and take her chances on escaping.

Comment

Medea's attitude towards her situation has, because of the additional penalty imposed on her by Creon, undergone a complete revolution. Whereas before she had thoughts of death, it was as much her own death as that of Jason she desired; and she had no thoughts of murder. But the lovesick Medea has vanished and she now stands forth as the sorceress of old, as she coldly plans not only murder but her getaway as well.

First Stasimon (410-445)

The Chorus say that the way of the world is being reversed and that women are finally coming into their own; no longer will they be slandered for their faithlessness. Jason's behavior proves that the old oaths are honored no longer by men.

Second Episode (446-626)

Jason enters and Medea comes out of the house. He accuses her of causing her own banishment by threatening Creon's family, and wants to make some financial arrangements for her exile. Medea says his coming to see her proves that he's reached the lowest possible condition: he no longer feels shame. She recites the crimes she committed to help him, crimes which have cut her off from any possibility of receiving refuge with her family. He hasn't even the excuse that she has not borne him children, to justify his new marriage.

Jason maintains that she overrates her help to him and underrates the blessing he bestowed by bringing her to such a civilized country as Greece. He is remarrying, he says, to gain wealth and power for her and ford their children-not because he doesn't love her or because he loves the princess. She answers that, had he really put the interests of his family first, he would have consulted her first, and not made a secret match. She refuses his help and tells him to go; he's left his bride alone too long.

Comment

A striking characteristic of Euripides' plays is the use of argumentative rhetoric. The speeches by Jason and Medea are of nearly identical length, and the arguments of one are answered by the other, as in a formal debate. The Chorus accuse Jason of using a specious art, and he clearly loses the debate. His arguments, however, have served to further delineate his character, revealing his ambition for wealth and power, and his cowardliness.

But however balanced the speeches are as to length and arguments, there is a striking contrast between them in tone. Medea is furious; Jason is the rationalist par excellence. He can even rationalize irrationally: "You helped only because you were in love with me. What else could you have done?" Try to imagine Medea raging about the stage as Jason coldly represents all the advantages of his marriage to Glauke ("Calm down" he tells her at 1. 550).

Second Stasimon (627-662)

The Chorus say that love, when too powerful, brings misfortune: they hope to love moderately. Contemplating Medea, they hope that they will never find themselves away from friends and family, in a foreign land.

Third Episode (663-823)

Aegeus, King of Athens, enters. He is on his way to Athens, having been to consult the oracle of Apollo to discover why he is childless. After telling Aegeus her troubles Medea promises to cure his childlessness by her magic if he will give her refuge in Athens. He promises, with the qualification that she will have to get to Athens by herself; taking her might antagonize his friends in Corinth. Not satisfied with a promise, Medea makes him swear an oath never to surrender her to her enemies.

Comment

Aristotle criticized this scene with Aegeus for being unreasonable without justification (Poetics, ch. 25). But Aegeus not only provides her with promise of refuge but it is he who first plants the seeds in her mind of killing her children when he bemoans his own childlessness.

After Aegeus leaves, she tells the Chorus that she now has a real chance of success. She confides her plan of revenge to them: she will send for Jason and sweetly beg that he keep the children. They will take a robe and a headdress as gifts for the king's daughter; wearing them, she, and anyone who touches her, will die. Medea plans then to kill her children, leaving Jason childless. The Chorus try, but fail, to dissuade her. She sends the Nurse to summon Jason.

Third Stasimon (824-865)

The Chorus sing a tribute to Athens, praising its gentle climate and the fame it has won for its sacred streams and as the birthplace of the nine Muses. (The Muses are divine figures representing the fine arts: music, painting, poetry, etc.) How, the Chorus wonder, can such a city welcome the murderess of her own children? The Chorus express amazement that Medea can look on her children and yet retain her bloody purpose.

Comment

This celebrated choral ode in praise of Athens, and the scene with Aegeus that precedes it, have been criticized as unmotivated and irrelevant to the play. Yet Aegeus' unhappiness about his childlessness illustrates the effect Medea's revenge will have on Jason, who will lose both his children and his bride; a refuge is given to Medea, who throughout the play is a victim of isolation and loneliness; and the choral ode provides the only opportunity in the play for someone who knows Medea's plan to try to deter her.

A further justification (though not one based on artistic grounds) for this ode in praise of Athens is that since at the time of the production (431 B.C.) Athens was at the height of its political power and wealth, the audience would welcome a beautiful choral song that satisfied their feelings of Athens' superiority in the arts as well as in politics.

Fourth Episode (866-975)

Jason enters to confront a Medea feigning humility and regret for her earlier anger. She says she should have encouraged his new marriage and hopes that they can now be reconciled. He is glad she is finally being sensible. She asks him to keep the children in Corinth. He promises to do so, thinking he can probably persuade his new wife, at least. He goes out with the children, who carry the robe and golden headdress for his bride.

Fourth Stasimon (976-1001)

The Chorus say that any hope they had that the children might live is now gone, Jason's bride will inevitably try on the luxurious gifts and die. Their sympathy extends even to Jason, who little knows what **catastrophe** he brings to his bride and his children.

Fifth Episode (1002-1250)

The Tutor enters with Medea's children. The request has been granted, and the children may stay. The Tutor is dumbfounded by the moans with which Medea receives the news. Left alone with the children, Medea decides to spare their lives; then she changes her mind. Torn by the conflict between love for them and desire for revenge, she sends them into the house, then calls them back again to fondle them. She says she now understands the terrible nature of the deed she's about to perform, but will not turn back. Her passion, she says, is stronger than her reason.

Comment

In this scene Medea fully comprehends what she is about to do and makes her tragic decision. In a sense, the whole conflict of the play is within Medea herself. And the sense of tragedy is heightened when we see that Medea herself is aware of this irrationality within her that leads her on to do evil. "I know the wickedness of what I Plan, but my (irrational) fury is stronger than my purpose, fury, which is the greatest cause of man's evils" (11. 1078-80). When permission is granted for the children to remain, her suffering is intensified; but that permission was granted to a Medea who does not exist: a disguised Medea helping the real Medea to gain her revenge. Her love of her children makes her sympathetic, human, tragic-but her love of Jason and her humiliation at his desertion touch her deepest and strongest feelings.

Fifth Stasimon (1251-1292)

The Chorus say that, though women, they are not incapable of wisdom, and assert that childless people are happiest. Children may grow up to be blessings or curses and, even if they turn out well, may die, and what misfortune is worse than that?

Exodos (1293-1419)

A Messenger comes from the palace to warn Medea to flee; the princess and Creon have been killed by her magic. She is exultant and tells him not to talk so fast; she wants to hear every detail of their suffering. When the children arrived, he says, the household was happy to see the quarrel between Jason and Medea ended. Although the princess was displeased to see the children, she changed when she saw their gifts. Putting them on, she walked to the mirror. The garments burst into flames and she sank to the ground; the servants ran in distraction through the house. Creon came in to find his daughter dead and, throwing himself on her body, was engulfed by the flames, unable to pull away.

Medea goes into the house to kill her children immediately, lest someone come from the palace and kill them. Cries are heard within the house and the Chorus lament the murder, saying that only one other woman, the mad Ino, ever killed her own children.

Jason comes looking for the children, afraid someone from the palace will seek vengeance on him and on them. The Chorus tell him they are dead, and he rushes to the doors of the house. Medea appears above the house in a chariot drawn by dragons; the bodies of the children are beside her. She taunts Jason, saying he'll never be able to reach her. He reproaches himself for not having realized what a monster she was after the first crimes she committed for him. Medea is triumphant; she knows she has touched his heart at last. His love, she tells him, was too feeble; this is his punishment. He begs to bury his children, to at least be allowed to touch or kiss them. Medea refuses to give him any comfort whatsoever and departs in the chariot.

Comment

Aristotle also criticized this last scene, this time accusing Euripides of introducing a supernatural element which does not arise naturally from the plot (Poetics, ch. 15); many later critics have concurred with this view. If, however, the **episode** is considered in light of the **theme** of the play, and not just the plot alone, it is shown to be a brilliant close to the play.

To say that the **theme** of *Medea* is revenge is to look only at the plot. The real conflict in the play is between the forces of rationality and irrationality, or, if you will, between the mind and the heart-a **theme** that is to return in *Hippolytus* and the *Bacchae,* among other plays of Euripides. Jason is purely rational (and is very much representative of many of Euripides' contemporaries); Medea is more human in that she is both rational and irrational and struggles to attain some balance within herself (as the Chorus seem to have done). But the irrational wins out and the formal expression of this is the chariot with all of its **connotations** of the supernatural.

THE PLAYS OF EURIPIDES

HIPPOLYTUS

BACKGROUND

Euripides won only four first prizes in his life at the dramatic festivals; one of these was for *Hippolytus* and the three plays accompanying. He had written an earlier *Hippolytus* dealing with the same story but with a much different emphasis which not only did not win him a prize, but angered the Athenians with its harsh portrayal of Phaedra. In this first version (sometimes called *Hippolytus Veiled* to distinguish it from our play, which in turn is sometimes called *Hippolytus Crowned*) Phaedra portrayed more lust than love towards Hippolytus and probably offered herself to him in person rather than through the Nurse. Horrified at this proposal Hippolytus veiled his head (whence the variant title), causing Phaedra to seek revenge for herself alone, not for the sake of her children. She made up a story of rape which brought Hippolytus in conflict with Theseus, who exiled his son. This led to his death, just as it does in our play. Somehow Phaedra's story was revealed as a lie and she committed suicide. Sophocles also wrote a play based on this story, the Phaedra. There is less evidence for this play than for *Hippolytus Veiled*, but it seems sure that Phaedra was here given a nobler character (for example, she made known her love to Hippolytus only because she thought Theseus was dead and that therefore there was nothing wrong in her actions). This play may well have been written after *Hippolytus Veiled* and before the *Hippolytus Crowned*, but this is only a guess. (There also were a third century B.C. *Hippolytus* by Lycophron, a first century A.D. *Phaedra* by Seneca, a seventeenth century French *Phèdre* by Racine, and a recent movie, *Phaedra*, all dealing with this same story (in the movie a fast sports car is substituted for Hippolytus' chariot).

King Theseus once attacked the Amazons and carried off their queen, Antiope, by whom he had an illegitimate son, Hippolytus. Later he married Phaedra, who became his queen in Troezen. He sent Hippolytus to live with his grandfather Pittheus, the king of Troezen, so that there would be no conflict between Hippolytus and the legitimate children of Phaedra.

CHARACTERS

Aphrodite: Goddess of love, enemy of Artemis, she seeks revenge on Hippolytus for his dedication to Artemis.

Artemis: Goddess of chastity and of the hunt; enemy of Aphrodite, she defends Hippolytus.

Theseus: King of Troezen, father of Hippolytus.

Phaedra: Wife of Theseus, stepmother of Hippolytus.

Hippolytus: Son of Theseus and Antiope, dedicated to chastity.

Attendants: Companions of Hippolytus.

Chorus: Young married women of Troezen.

Nurse: Companion of Phaedra.

Messenger

SETTING

In front of the palace of King Theseus in Troezen, a city on the coast of the Saronic Gulf, about thirty miles south of Athens; a statue of Aphrodite is on one side of the main entrance (1. 101) and there is also either a status or altar of Artemis (11. 58ff., 1092ff.), but its position is not made clear by the text. Most people consider it to have been a statue placed symmetrically with respect to the statue of Aphrodite on the other side of the door.

Prologue (1-120)

The goddess Aphrodite claims great power and respect among both gods and men. Only Hippolytus despises her, scorns love, and refuses marriage. Instead of honoring love, as a young man should, he honors Artemis, the virgin goddess, and spends his time hunting. Aphrodite has prepared her revenge by making Phaedra, his stepmother, fall in love with him. The first time Phaedra saw him she fell so deeply in love that she had a temple built for Aphrodite in his honor. She has kept her love secret and is wasting away, but no one knows what disease affects her. Aphrodite plans that Theseus shall discover her passion and, with one of the three wishes given him by Poseidon, shall kill Hippolytus. Phaedra shall die too, but honorably; her suffering must be less than that of Aphrodite's enemies.

Comment

This extremely detailed description of what will happen in the play probably is intended to do more than give dramatic **irony** to succeeding scenes. It has been conjectured that Euripides' earlier play on this subject was criticized on the grounds that Phaedra's passion for Hippolytus was distasteful to the audience. In this version, by making Aphrodite the instigator who takes total responsibility, Euripides makes Phaedra an unwilling instrument of Aphrodite's revenge. It also keeps the focus of the play firmly on Hippolytus; later dramatists make Phaedra the main character-in fact, use her name for the title.

On a symbolic level Aphrodite represents the natural force of love. By not worshipping her as a goddess Hippolytus denies this force in himself, just as Pentheus in the *Bacchae* refuses to believe in Dionysus and hence in all that Dionysus represents.

Seeing Hippolytus and his attendants returning from the hunt, Aphrodite vanishes. Hippolytus proposes that he and his friends sing to Artemis. After they have praised her as the most beautiful of goddesses, Hippolytus offers her a wreath, which he says came from a meadow so pure that it has never been cut by a scythe or fed the flocks of a shepherd. Only those who have avoided the wicked world and avoided all temptations can pick the flowers there. One of the attendants reminds Hippolytus that there is another goddess, Aphrodite, whose service he has neglected. Hippolytus disdainfully avoids her altar; he doesn't like gods who enjoy being worshipped at night. The leader suggests that mortals ought to accept what is given by the gods, but Hippolytus merely bids Aphrodite "a long farewell." They all go to dine except the leader, who prays to Aphrodite that she forgive the youthful impetuousness of Hippolytus.

Comment

Hippolytus' pride in his chastity is evident in his scornful treatment of the goddess Aphrodite. As a representative of adolescent fanaticism, Hippolytus is perhaps unrivaled in dramatic literature. Although emphasis has been placed on his alleged priggishness, much can also be said about qualities which make him appealing to the audience, even before their sympathy is aroused by the unjust accusation later in the play. Dedication to chastity as a principle of life has a long history in civilization, and in association with Hippolytus' youth, handsomeness, and almost excessive vitality, it is shorn of its drearier associations. Further, the existence of Artemis as goddess of chastity postulates at least the theory of dedication to her worship. Of course, the Greek virtue of the "golden mean," or moderation, would recommend the avoidance of either extreme.

Parodos (121-169)

The Chorus of fifteen women of Troezen come in. They have heard that their queen is wasting away from sickness, refusing food, and near death. They offer several suggestions to explain her illness: she is possessed by Pan or Hecate or the Corybantes or the Mountain Mother (Cybele); she has heard that Theseus is having an affair with another woman; she has had some bad news given her; or she is pregnant and feeling ill from this. The Chorus themselves have given birth and know what it is like.

They express thanks that Artemis, who oversees childbirth, is kind to them.

Comment

Note that each of the reasons they suggest for Phaedra's illness has some element of truth in it. That they don't think of the real reasons is some suggestion of the monstrousness of Phaedra's love for Hippolytus.

Artemis is traditionally the goddess of childbirth, but Euripides could easily have ignored all reference to this function of hers. To have the Chorus mention that Artemis, the virgin goddess, eases the labor pains of women is to hint that Hippolytus, with his strict chastity, goes even further than the goddess in whose name he observes his chastity.

First Episode (170-524)

The Nurse brings out Phaedra, who lies on a couch, and tells the Chorus Phaedra will probably want to go inside immediately, she's become so changeable. The Nurse complains about her job, saying it's better to be sick than to care for the sick-that gives you two people's suffering. She morbidly laments the never-ending unhappiness of life.

Phaedra, raving wildly, longs to drink spring water, to ride wild horses, and go to the mountains to join the hunt. The Nurse, very down to earth, tells her there's a perfectly good stream just beside the palace. Speaking more quietly, Phaedra realizes she has been raving; ashamed, she asks the Nurse to cover her head.

Comment

Because the audience has been fully apprized of the situation by Aphrodite, it understands Phaedra's wild wishes as indirect expressions of her desire to be with Hippolytus. Seeing her nearly mad, the audience holds her less responsible for her passion, and seeing her shame when she recovers herself, less reprehensible.

The Nurse covers Phaedra as requested, and then wonders when the earth will ever cover her. She sententiously generalizes about her hard lot: she says that having to grieve for two people, as she does, is an example of excess, which is bad for the health.

Comment

Throughout the play, the Nurse provides an effective contrast to Phaedra. Being a servant, she can be represented as crude, practical, insensitive, and complaining. The contrast is so great that it frequently approaches comedy. The effect on the stage would depend on the way the actor played the role. She is an example of a stock stage character which finds its culmination in the Nurse in Shakespeare's Romeo and Juliet.

In an exchange with the Chorus, the Nurse says that Theseus is now away from home. She is urged by the Chorus to press further her inquiries into the cause of Phaedra's illness. She tells Phaedra that, if she dies, she will betray her children, for the throne of Troezen will go to Hippolytus. At the mention of his name, Phaedra starts up and forbids it to be mentioned. After insistent pleading from the Nurse, she agrees to tell her trouble. Love, Phaedra says, has been the undoing of her whole family:

her mother, Pasiphae, loved a bull, her sister a god. When the Nurse discovers Phaedra's love for Hippolytus, she is horrified; she says that such a wicked passion will destroy them all.

The Nurse throws herself to the ground, temporarily withdrawing from the action. (This is more likely than the suggestion of some, that she leaves at this point and returns at line 433.)

Phaedra tells the Chorus she has done everything to fight her passion: she hid her thoughts from others; she learned to endure them; she finally decided to die. Her desire for virtue has always been stronger than the involuntary passion consuming her. In reply, the Nurse apologizes for her earlier outburst; since Phaedra is strong, Aphrodite has afflicted her powerfully, and this explains the extent of her sickness. She is aiming at too great a perfection in her life; what she needs now is not a solemn speech but a man! Phaedra forbids her to ever say anything like that again, but the Nurse continues, arguing that this is not a matter of self-indulgence, but of life and death. The Nurse then says she has just remembered a magic potion which will help to soothe Phaedra's suffering. Phaedra is suspicious but finally agrees to try it; she absolutely forbids the nurse to mention any of this to Hippolytus.

Comment

In Euripides' day there was a discussion raging between the partisans of nomos (law) and those of physis (nature). The more conservative f the Greeks thought that society had to be based on law in order to function properly. Socrates was one such person and his teachings on government are found reflected in the works of his pupil Plato (especially the Gorgias and the

Republic). Perhaps the most expressive statement of the other side's views is found in Aristophanes' Clouds (line 1078): "Enjoy your nature, be unruly, have fun, think nothing shameful." The Nurse, telling Phaedra that she should do nothing else than give in to her passion, sets herself firmly on the side of the defenders of physis.

First Stasimon (525-564)

The Chorus sing to Love, which in his soft moods brings sweet desire, but in angry moods is destructive. They refer to the stories of Iole and of Semele as examples of love's destructive effects.

Second Episode (565-731)

Phaedra, standing by the door of the palace, is listening to the conversation within the house; she hears Hippolytus calling the Nurse a pimp and traitor. He then bursts out of the door, closely followed by the Nurse, entreating him to observe his oath of silence. He says he made the oath with his tongue, not his heart.

Comment

Since Hippolytus makes no reference to Phaedra's presence we must imagine her off to the side, where she can hear Hippolytus and the Nurse, but where she would be overlooked by Hippolytus as he hurries out of the palace. A place that meets these requirements and would have further dramatic force is alongside the statue of Aphrodite.

Hippolytus blurted out in anger that his tongue made the oath, not his heart, but in point of fact he does feel bound by it, as he says later on in this scene, and as is made clear by his refusal to tell his father what he knows even though his sentence of exile hangs on it. This line was quoted out of context by Aristophanes (*Frogs*, 11. 101, 1471, Thesmophoriazusae, 1.275) to make it appear as if this was a sentiment that Euripides himself approved of.

Hippolytus delivers a long tirade against women. Zeus, he says, created the world badly when he ordained that women should be necessary for a man to have children. Children should be bought in the temple. Fathers happily pay a dower to get rid of daughters. Husbands find their own wealth squandered for fancy clothes. The best wife is a stupid wife; a clever one only thinks up villainy. Servants are worse, if possible, than wives; they should be kept penned up with the beasts so they won't hear and spread abroad the wickedness of wives.

He says that an affair with Phaedra would be an outrage on his father's honor; he feels polluted by its very mention. He plans to go away until his father returns. Then he'll observe Phaedra's audacity by watching her manner when she greets him. He intends to hate women until someone can prove they have self-control.

Phaedra curses the Nurse for meddling, and the Nurse blandly replies that had she succeeded, she would have been considered a very wise woman indeed; she adds bitterly that wisdom is measured by success. Phaedra says she will arrange her own affairs and sends the Nurse away. After binding the Chorus to a promise that they will never reveal what they have heard, Phaedra tells them she will commit suicide in such a manner as to teach Hippolytus a lesson. She goes into the house to carry out her plan.

Second Stasimon (732-775)

The Chorus wish they could go to some distant land. They feel that evil was on board the ship that brought Phaedra to Troezen, there to commit suicide to preserve her donor.

Third Episode (776-1101)

The Nurse runs out of the house shouting that Phaedra has hanged herself. Unnoticed, Theseus has returned and inquires about the uproar coming from the house. The Chorus say that Phaedra has hanged herself. They themselves, they tell Theseus, have just arrived to mourn for her, and that is all they know. Theseus commands that the doors be opened, and through the use of the eccyclema(see the General Introduction), Phaedra's body is stretched out before everyone's eyes. The Chorus, and Theseus then with them, lament her death until Theseus notices a letter clutched in her hand.

In it she wrote that Hippolytus had raped her. In a rage at this violation of honor, Theseus prays that one of the three wishes granted him by Poseidon be fulfilled that day: he asks for the death of Hippolytus. Hippolytus returns and innocently asks the cause of Phaedra's death. He is, at first, dismayed by Theseus' generalizations about the way men are betrayed by those they think their friends. Then Theseus turns the argument against Hippolytus, and tells him what the letter contained. Is not Phaedra's accusation proved true by her suicide? He taunts Hippolytus for feeling a false sense of superiority because he is a vegetarian and a reader of scholarly books, accuses him of hypocrisy and banishes him.

Comment

In the prologue, Aphrodite characterized Hippolytus' hunting as an attempt to clear the forest of wild beasts. Now we learn from Theseus that Hippolytus does not eat any of the animals he kills, and that he spends his time alone reading. In other words, Hippolytus is remarkably like many monks, who swear themselves to chastity, abstain from meat, and devote themselves to reading.

Hippolytus' answer to his father's charges is more formal argument than passionate denial; he pleads his religious dedication to chastity, his straightforward manner, his lack of ambition for the throne, and Phaedra's plain appearance. Theseus will neither allow Hippolytus' oath to be tested nor seers to be consulted, and reaffirms Hippolytus' banishment.

Comment

Hippolytus' lack of passion in his arguments can partly be attributed to Euripides' characteristic use of formal argument in his plays; it is also appropriate to Hippolytus' character.

The serious regard Greek society held for oaths explains why Hippolytus does not defend himself by repeating what the Nurse told hit, not that his father would believe him. He would have believed the Chorus, but they too respect their oath of silence. Of course, had they broken the oath, Theseus would learn they had lied to him earlier, when they said they didn't know what had happened. Theseus might therefore refuse to believe their altered story and subsequent action would remain the same. After the false accusation by Phaedra and the violent reaction of Theseus, Hippolytus has the audience's sympathy.

Third Stasimon (1102-1150)

The Chorus say that contemplation of the gods reveals soothing order, but contemplation of men only restless change. Doubts fill their minds at the sight of a so much admired young man being driven from his home.

Comment

The Chorus lament only the sentence of exile, seeming to have forgotten that Theseus asked Poseidon for his death. But their mention of the "currents of life," sands of the seashore, and Hippolytus' chariot and horses are particularly ominous in light of what they learn immediately afterwards.

THE PLAYS OF EURIPIDES

HERACLEIDAE

BACKGROUND

The Heracleidae is a political play written to glorify Athens at a time when she was at war with Sparta. Suffering from serious dramatic flaws, the play has neither enjoyed popularity nor had much influence.

Zeus once visited Alcmene in the shape of her husband, Amphitryon, who was away from home. As a result of this visit she was to bear the child, Heracles: thus Zeus planned to father a hero who should rule over the race of Perseus, from whom both Alcmene and Amphitryon were descended. But Zeus' wife Hera delayed the birth of Heracles and hastened the birth of Eurystheus, a grandson of Perseus by another line of descent. Thus Eurystheus was born before Heracles, and Heracles lost the birthright Zeus had intended for him. When a grown man, Heracles went mad and killed his first wife, Megara, and their children. (See Euripides, *Heracles.*) As punishment, the oracle at Delphi ordered him to serve Eurystheus, who assigned him the famous "twelve labors." After the death of Heracles, Eurystheus tried to kill Heracles' children by Deianira, his second wife.

With Alcmene, Heracles' mother, they escaped and vainly sought refuge in one Greek state after another. Eurystheus has constantly pursued them.

CHARACTERS

Iolaus: A friend of Heracles.

Eurystheus: King of Argos, in pursuit of Heracles' children.

Copreus: A herald of Eurystheus.

Demophon: King of Athens, who gives refuge to Heracles' children.

Macaria: Daughter of Heracles who offers to sacrifice herself to the gods.

Alcmene: Mother of Heracles.

Servant: Of Hyllus, a son of Heracles.

Chorus: Old men of Athens.

Messenger

SETTING

In front of the altar and temple of Zeus at Marathon, a village on the coast 22 miles northeast of Athens.

An old friend of Heracles, Iolaus, says that he has come to Marathon with the mother and children of Heracles to seek refuge from the pursuit of Eurystheus. Copreus, a messenger from Eurystheus, arrives in pursuit of the children, whom he will take to Argos, where they will be killed. The old and feeble Iolaus fights with him and is thrown to the ground.

The Chorus of Athenian elders enter and demand to know the cause of the fight. After hearing both sides, they conclude that Copreus had no right to enter the country at all, much less attempt to violate a claim of sanctuary, without first informing the king of his presence and his mission.

The king of Athens, Demophon, enters and hears the arguments of both sides. He decides to give sanctuary to the suppliants even though it should mean war with Argos: the suppliants are at the altar of Zeus, they are related to him, and the reputation of Athens as a free city is at stake. The herald leaves and King Demophon prepares to raise an army and to meet the Argives. When the Argive army arrives, Demophon consults the oracles, who tell him to sacrifice a noble maiden to Demeter (goddess of agriculture and vegetation). This angers the Athenian citizens, who threaten civil war: why should they fight a war for foreigners, let alone make sacrifices to win such wars? Iolaus offers to give himself up to Eurystheus, but Demophon points out that this would not help: only the children are wanted, for they are a potential threat to Eurystheus' throne.

Macaria, a daughter of Heracles, offers to be the sacrifice Demeter has demanded. She argues that the children of Heracles cannot expect others to die for them if they are unwilling to die themselves. Iolaus wants her and her sisters to draw lots, but she insists on making a voluntary sacrifice and is led away.

Comment

An ancient summary attached to the manuscript of this play says that Macaria was honored for having died bravely, but this does not appear in the text of our play. It has been thought, therefore, that a scene describing the death of Macaria, and (perhaps) a following choral ode, were at some very early date excised. This would also explain the very short length of the play. In addition, ancient commentators quote lines from *The Heracleidae* which do not appear in our text.

A servant of Hyllus, one of Heracles' sons, announces that Hyllus is nearby with a large army and intends to fight the invading Argives. The aged Iolaus prepares himself to join them by donning captured arms hanging in the temple, and, despite the servant's protest that he is too old, resolves to fight. He is able to get out of the temple only with the servant's help.

After the battle, the servant returns to announce that not only have the forces of Athens been triumphant, but the aged Iolaus was miraculously restored to his youth and fought like a great hero. When he first arrived on the battlefield, he had challenged Eurystheus to single combat, but had been refused because he was too old. The servant describes the rest of the battle in detail.

When Eurystheus is brought in as a prisoner, Alcmene wants to kill him in revenge, but she is told that Athenians do not kill prisoners taken alive in battle. Realizing that she is determined to kill him, one way or another, Eurystheus reveals an old prophecy that his spirit will always protect Athens from attacks by decendants of the children of Heracles, and that he is destined to be buried on Athenian soil. Hearing this, the Athenians consent to his death.

Comment

Athens was very proud of her ancient glories; this play argues that the sanctuary given to the children of Heracles years before proves Sparta to be wrong in fighting against Athens, for the Spartans are decendants of Heracles. The prophecy about the protective spirit of Eurystheus is a warning that Athens has the gods on her side. The play also praises Athenian justice and devoutness at a time when Athens had a bad reputation for exploiting her allies.

THE PLAYS OF EURIPIDES

ANDROMACHE

BACKGROUND

Andromache is a political, or propaganda, play attacking Sparta and the Delphic oracle of Apollo, which had predicted a Spartan victory in the Peloponnesian War. Much criticized for its lack of unity, the play has had little influence. It is, however, the source for Racine's play Andromaque.

Andromache, the widow of Hector, was given to Achilles' son Neoptolemus when the spoils of the Trojan War were divided. Neoptolemus made her his slave and concubine, and they had a son, Molossus. Later, Neoptolemus married Hermione-daughter of Menelaus and Helen-who had earlier been betrothed to Orestes, son of Menelaus' brother, Agamemnon.

CHARACTERS

Andromache: Widow of Hector, now slave-concubine to Neoptolemus.

Maid: To Andromache.

Molossus: Son of Andromache and Neoptolemus.

Menelaus: King of Sparta.

Hermione: Daughter of Menelaus and wife of Neoptolemus.

Nurse: Of Hermione.

Peleus: Father of Achilles.

Thetis: A sea-goddess, wife of Peleus and mother of Achilles.

Orestes: Son of Agamemnon.

Chorus: Of Women.

Messenger

SETTING

In front of the temple of Thetis, in Thessaly (the largest country in Greece; north of Athens). The palace of Achilles is nearby.

Andromache laments her present position as slave in Neoptolemus' household. She once hoped that their son Molossus would grow up to help improve her situation, but now Neoptolemus has married Hermione, who accuses Andromache of using magic to keep her from having children, and threatens to kill her. Andromache has come to the shrine of Thetis seeking sanctuary from Hermione and her father, Menelaus, who has come from Sparta to help his daughter get rid of Andromache. Andromache's maid comes to tell her that Menelaus and Hermione plan to kill Molossus, whom Andromache had sent away for safekeeping. She cannot appeal to Neoptolemus, for he has gone to the shrine of Apollo to beg forgiveness: he had offended the god by his sin of demanding satisfaction from Apollo for the death of his father, Achilles. Andromache has ordered messengers to go to the feeble King Peleus to beg for help, but they, fearing Hermione, have not left. Now she sends her maid on the same mission. The Chorus of women recommend that Andromache accept the fact she is a slave and leave the shrine.

Hermione enters the temple and accuses Andromache of trying to usurp her place. She threatens to kill her unless she serves as a slave should. Calling Andromache a wanton barbarian, she taunts her with having a child by the son of the man (Achilles) who killed her husband (Hector). Andromache replies by accusing Hermione of losing her husband's love by being a poor wife. Hermione vows to get Andromache out of the temple and kill her before Neoptolemus returns.

The Chorus lament the day Paris (who stole Helen and started the Trojan War) was allowed to live: his mother had been warned he would cause trouble for Troy.

Menelaus has discovered where Molossus, Andromache's son, was hidden and brings him in. Unless Andromache leaves her sanctuary in the temple, he will be killed. She warns Menelaus of the consequences to Hermione if Neoptolemus returns and finds his son dead. Menelaus answers that Andromache is only a slave and, as such, subject to his orders. She surrenders herself to save her son, and Menelaus immediately retracts his promise. Hermione can decide whether or not Molossus shall live. He is not ashamed of his treachery and Andromache says that all Spartans behave dishonorably.

Comment

The treachery of Menelaus and the speech of Andromache are intended to vilify Sparta, Athens' enemy in the Peloponnesian War.

The Chorus say that rival wives and sons of different mothers always cause unhappiness.

Andromache and her son are being led out to be killed when King Peleus enters and demands that Andromache be freed: Menelaus defies him. Peleus delivers a diatribe against Sparta, saying that all their women are wantons, and that Menelaus himself was a weakling not to have killed Helen when he got her back. They argue at length, and when Peleus unties the bonds of Andromache, Menelaus does not stop him. After Neoptolemus' return, Menelaus is resolved to state his case before him.

The Nurse of Hermione tells the Chorus that her mistress is threatening suicide, for she is afraid Neoptolemus will return and punish her. In a wild state, her clothes loose, Hermione enters with a sword in her hand, which the Nurse takes from her.

Comment

The dress of Hermione here is usually considered to be an attack on what Athens regarded to be Spartan immorality in feminine dress.

Orestes enters, having come to visit his cousin, Hermione. She tells him her fears, blaming her actions on women friends who inflame her jealousy. She adds that no house should allow outside women even to visit, for they stir up trouble. The Chorus say women should not malign one another. Orestes reminds her that she was once engaged to him and that only her father's treachery led to her present marriage. His real reason for being there, he says, is to take her away with him. Hermione is anxious to leave Neoptolemus now, and they leave together, but not before Orestes states that he has brought false accusations which will cause Apollo to kill Neoptolemus.

King Peleus enters, having heard of Hermione's flight, and learns that it is Orestes who has taken her. He is about to inform Neoptolemus of the plot against him when a Messenger brings in news of Neoptolemus' death. In Delphi, Orestes had spread a rumor that Neoptolemus was there to steal the gold from the temple. The townspeople attacked him but he, though wounded, had fought them off. Then a voice had come from the temple urging the people to attack again. This time he was killed.

Comment

This scene is intended to malign the Delphic oracle, which was against the Athenians in the Peloponnesian War. The Thessalians (descendants of Achilles) were friendly to Athens; hence the kindly treatment of Peleus and his family throughout the play.

The body of Neoptolemus is carried in and the Chorus mourn his death.

From above, the goddess Thetis appears and proclaims that Andromache is to marry Helenus (Hector's brother) in the city of Molossus, where her son will carry on the family line. Peleus will be transformed into a god and will dwell with his wife, the goddess Thetis.

THE PLAYS OF EURIPIDES

HECUBA

BACKGROUND

During the Trojan War, the Queen of Troy, Hecuba, sent her young son, Polydorus, to stay with Polymestor, king of Thrace, where he would be safe. A large sum of money was entrusted to Polymestor so the boy would not be poverty-stricken if the Trojans lost the war. After the Greeks defeated the Trojans, Polymestor killed Polydorus in order to get his money. The Trojan women were divided among the victorious Greeks after the war, and Hecuba was given to Agamemnon, leader of the Greek forces.

CHARACTERS

The Ghost Of Polydorus: Son of Hecuba and Priam, King of Troy.

Hecuba: Wife of Priam: given to Agmemnon after the Trojan War.

Chorus: Captive Trojan women.

Polyxena: Daughter of Hecuba and Priam.

Odysseus: King of Ithaca, most famous for his wanderings as he attempted to return home after the Trojan War.

Talthybius: A herald of Agamemnon.

Maid. Of Hecuba.

Agamemnon: Leader of the Greek forces in the Trojan War.

Polymestor: King of Thrace, blinded by Hecuba and the women.

Children: Of Polymestor.

Attendants

SETTING

In front of Agamemnon's tent in the Thracian peninsula, across the Hellespont from Troy.

The Ghost of Polydorus appears and tells how Priam sent the living Polydorus to Polymestor's house, and how he was killed and thrown into the sea when Polymestor heard that the Trojans had lost the war. The Ghost explains that the Greeks are in Thrace now because the spirit of Achilles has demanded the sacrifice of Polyxena, Polydorus' sister, before the ships will have a favorable wind to sail with. The Ghost vanishes.

From the tent of Agamemnon comes the aged Queen of Troy, Hecuba, supported by her attendants. She is unaware as yet of her son's murder or of the demand of Achilles' spirit, but she has had dreams which frighten her. Her fears become specific when the Chorus of captive Trojan women enter to tell her Polyxena must be sacrificed. When Polyxena is told, she is chiefly concerned for her mother, who has already suffered so much.

Official news of the sacrifice is brought by Odysseus, and Hecuba reminds him that she saved his life when he came as a spy to Troy during the war. She begs for her daughter's life as he had once begged for his, but Odysseus is adamant.

When Polyxena comes out, she says she would rather die than live the life of a slave; she discourages Hecuba's desire to die with her. After Odysseus and his attendants have led Polyxena away, the Trojan women lament to leave Asia and wonder where they will be taken.

The herald Talthybius comes seeking Hecuba; the sacrifice is over and she is to bury her daughter's body. He tells Hecuba that at the sacrifice Polyxena refused to be held by the soldiers, saying she wanted to die willingly. Tearing her robe from her shoulders, she exposed her neck and breast and told the son of Achilles to strike wherever he chose.

The herald has no sooner left than the body of Hecuba's son, Polydorus, is brought in, having been found washed up on the shore. When Agamemnon comes in to see what is delaying Hecuba, she begs him to avenge Polydorus' death. He is reluctant because the men of the army consider Polymestor their friend. Hecuba says she will get her own revenge if Agamemnon will only keep the Greeks from interfering.

Hecuba sends an attendant to tell Polymestor to come with his children; she has a message for them. They arrive and

Polymestor offers his condolences at the fall of Troy. He says that her son, Polydorus, is well. She tells him that the Trojans have buried gold near a temple of Athena, and that she wants both him and his children to know about it so they can tell her son. She says there is also gold in the tent, and he goes in with the children. Inside the tent, Hecuba and the Trojan women blind Polymestor and kill his children.

Agamemnon, hearing Polymestor's cries, comes in and listens to the arguments of Hecuba and the man she blinded. Polymestor pleads that he killed Polydorus lest he should found another Trojan race, thus bringing the anger of the Greeks on Thrace, which sheltered Polydorus. Hecuba argues that he killed for the gold, and Agamemnon believes her. Polymestor repeats the prophecies of a Thracian seer, who said that Hecuba would be transformed into a dog and would jump into the sea, and that Agamemnon and Cassandra would be slain by Clytemnestra, Agamemnon's wife, when he arrived home. Agamemnon banishes Polymestor to a desert island and the Greeks prepare to sail for home.

Comment

Although *Hecuba* suffers from lack of unity, the first part being concerned with the sacrifice of Polyxena, and the second with Hecuba's revenge, it maintains Hecuba in the forefront throughout. The profound grief of Hecuba, which fills the opening scenes of the play, is transformed into near triumph after she exacts her terrible revenge and is found justified by Agamemnon. Rhetoricians have greatly admired the *Hecuba* for its many excellent argumentative speeches and its intellectuality. The prophecy of the seer, repeated by Polymestor, takes the place of the **deus ex machina** (see General Introduction).

THE PLAYS OF EURIPIDES

CYCLOPS, A SATYR-PLAY

BACKGROUND

Cyclops is the only complete satyr-play to have survived. For characteristics of the satyr-play, see General Introduction. The story is based on Odysseus' encounter with the Cyclops, Polyphemus, in the ninth book of the *Odyssey*. The Chorus of Satyrs and the character of Silenus are Euripides' innovations, but the events of the play see no other great changes in the Homeric version.

CHARACTERS

Silenus: An old servant of the Cyclops.

Chorus: Satyrs, men usually represented with pointed ears, short horns, and goat legs. Attendants on Bacchus (Dionysus), god of wine, they are fond of riotous living and lechery.

Odysseus: Hero of the *Odyssey*, one of the Greek leaders in the Trojan War.

Cyclops: Named Polyphemus, a giant with only one eye-in the middle of his forehead.

Companions Of Odysseus

SETTING

In front of the cave of the Cyclops, at the foot of Mount Aetna in Sicily.

Silenus is cleaning the ground with a rake. He addresses Dionysus, saying it's the god's fault that he has to labor as a slave, instead of enjoying the revels of the Dionysian worship. Silenus had once set out with his children, the Satyrs, to search for Dionysus and had been shipwrecked on the Cyclops' coast and captured.

The Satyrs come back from the fields with the Cyclops' sheep, and Odysseus enters, seeking food for his men. Silenus tells him of monsters that inhabit the land, but cheers up considerably when Odysseus offers wine in exchange for food. Because the Cyclops does not cultivate the grape, Silenus has developed a considerable thirst and resolves to steal food from Polyphemus to exchange. Just then the Cyclops returns and sees Odysseus and his men. Silenus runs into the cave and comes out wrapped in bandages; he says he was injured by Odysseus and his companions, who tried to steal the Cyclops' sheep. Both Odysseus and the Chorus say he's lying, but the Cyclops believes him.

Odysseus begs to be spared, arguing that he has preserved the temples of the gods, but the Cyclops says he only does what he pleases, regardless of gods or men-and now it pleases him to cook and eat Odysseus and his men. He drives them into the cave.

Odysseus comes out of the cave after a while and tells about the meal; the Cyclops has cooked and eaten two of Odysseus' fattest men. Odysseus has served him the meal, and afterwards given him wine, to which he was not accustomed. Now the Cyclops is drunk, and Odysseus proposes a plan to the Satyrs to blind him with a burning pointed timber.

The Cyclops and Silenus, both drunk, come out of the cave and continue drinking, Silenus managing to get about three times his share. Soon completely drunk, the Cyclops gets the impression that the ugly Silenus is the handsome Ganymede, begins fondling him, and carries him off to his cave.

When Odysseus prepares to drive the brand into the Cyclops' eye, the Chorus of Satyrs, who had promised to help, all suddenly develop sprains. Odysseus gets his own men to help him execute his purpose in the cave. Blinded, the enraged Cyclops rushes out to catch his torturers, but succeeds only in hitting himself on the rocks.

When Odysseus had arrived, he had told the Cyclops his name was Noman. Now he reveals his real name and the Cyclops recalls a prophecy that Odysseus would blind him; he says Odysseus will be punished by being kept from home for many years. The Satyrs then prepare to leave the island with Odysseus.

Comment

Clearly intended to offer an amusing contrast with the tragedies which preceded it, the Cyclops makes no pretensions at edification. The character of Odysseus, however, is not undignified, and in the comments of the Chorus and the Cyclops, Euripides inserts his frequently expressed dislike of Helen for causing the Trojan War.

THE PLAYS OF EURIPIDES

HERACLES

BACKGROUND

Euripides has modified the usual legends about Heracles in this play by inventing the threat of Lycus against Heracles' family, and by having Heracles brought to Athens near the end of his life.

CHARACTERS

Amphitryon: Husband of Alcmene, who was the mother of Heracles. (Heracles' father was Zeus.)

Megara: Wife of Heracles; daughter of Creon.

Heracles: Son of Zeus and Alcmene.

Lycus: Unlawful king of Thebes; he overthrew Creon.

Theseus: King of Athens brought back from Hades by Heracles.

Iris: A messenger of the gods.

Madness: A divine figure who causes madness in men.

Chorus: Old men of Thebes.

Sons Of Heracles

SETTING

Before the place of Heracles at Thebes, about forty miles north of Athens. Nearby is an altar of Zeus.

In a prologue filled with genealogical detail, Amphitryon outlines the ancestral history of Heracles' and Lycus' families. Lycus is ruling Thebes unlawfully and is about to kill Amphitryon, and-because Megara is the daughter of the lawful king Creon-Heracles' wife Megara and their children. Heracles cannot help his family, for he is in Hades engaged in the last of his twelve labors: bringing back the monstor Cerberus who guards the gates there. The family have taken refuge at the altar of Zeus; they are forbidden to enter their palace and are watched too closely for escape.

The Chorus sympathize with them and encourage them, but, being old men, are unable to help. Lycus comes to ask how long they are going to try and prolong their lives by clinging to the altar. He claims that Heracles has been killed in Hades and will never help them. He justifies the proposed slaughter, claiming that Heracles' children will attempt to avenge their grandfather, Creon, by killing Lycus when they grow up. He depreciates the deeds of Heracles, calling him a coward for using a bow instead of a spear. Amphitryon, point by point, argues the other side and asks permission for them to go into exile. Lycus declares that he is through with words and orders his men to bring logs, stack them around the altar, and burn the suppliants alive.

Megara refuses to be burned alive: that is a coward's death. She has given up hope for Heracles' return and gets permission from Lycus to dress the children in robes of death to face their executioners. The old men of the Chorus have stoutly defended Heracles' family, but, because of their age, can do more than disagree with Lycus and sing in praise of Heracles' famous labors.

Megara returns with the children, dressed for death. She tells of the kingdoms Heracles had planned to give each of them and of the brides she intended them to marry. As Amphitryon laments the futility of the life he has lived, Megara catches sight of Heracles approaching. When Heracles hears the story of Creon's overthrow and Lycus' plan to kill Megara and the children, he resolves upon revenge. He tells them the reason for his long absence is that in addition to bringing Cerberus back from Hades and imprisoning him, he also brought back Theseus, who is now on his way to his home in Athens. With the children clinging to his robes, he goes into the palace with Megara.

Lycus returns and, impatient at finding only Amphitryon ready, storms into the palace to get the others. He is met inside by Heracles, and killed. The Chorus sing a joyful song of celebration, but it is interrupted by the appearance of Iris and Madness, hovering over the house.

Iris announces that she has come to make Heracles kill his own children by driving him mad. Hera, Zeus' wife, is behind the plan: she has hated Heracles since birth because Zeus was his father. She also resents his god-like strength and wants to humble him.

Comment

Like many of Euripides' plays, this one falls into two parts. Having been raised to the height of triumph when he kills Lycus, Heracles is now driven to the depths of despair by Madness. There is no real connection between the two parts, and for this reason, the play is often criticized for lack of unity.

A Messenger reports that when the fit of madness fell on Heracles, he believed he had to kill Eurystheus, the king who assigned his labors. Moving from room to room, he fancied that he was going from country to country. When Amphitryon tried to stop him, he thought it was Eurystheus, and his own children those of Eurystheus. In his madness he killed his three sons and his wife. When he threatened Amphitryon, Athena struck him and he fell asleep. The palace doors are opened to reveal Heracles, now asleep and tied to a pillar, surrounded by the bodies of his wife and children. When he wakes up, Amphitryon tells him what he has done; in his shame he wants to commit suicide.

Theseus, king of Athens, whom Heracles had freed from Hades, enters; he has heard that Lycus had overthrown Creon and desires to help overthrow Lycus. When he hears what Heracles has done, he asks him to uncover his head. Friendship, Theseus says, is greater than any fear he has of pollution from someone guilty of kindred bloodshed. Heracles, not easily comforted, says he can be welcome to no man; it would be better for him to commit suicide. Theseus offers him hospitality in Athens and half his wealth. He argues that even the gods commit evil acts, such as forbidden marriages, yet continue to live on Olympus and face out their crimes. Why shouldn't Heracles? Heracles vehemently denies this line of argument: such stories of the gods, he says, are merely the inventions of poets. A deity, if really such, can have no desires. Finally convinced that it would be cowardly to commit suicide, he resolves to go to Athens with Theseus. The law forbids him to remain in Thebes or even attend the funeral of his wife and children. He asks his father to bury his dead, and, leaning on Theseus, leaves.

Comment

Courage and nobility are the **themes** of this play. Megara in the first half of the play and Heracles in the second are innocent victims of powerful, authoritative forces they cannot defeat.

THE PLAYS OF EURIPIDES

SUPPLIANTS

BACKGROUND

Polyneices and Eteocles, sons of Oedipus, were to have shared the kingdom of Thebes, but Eteocles banished Polyneices. To regain his rights, Polyneices joined Adrastus, king of Argos, in an attack on Thebes. In the battle both Polyneices and Eteocles were killed. (See Euripides' *Phoenissae*.) Creon, who succeeded to the throne of Thebes, forbade the burial of Polyneices' body and the bodies of the other Argive heroes. (See Aeschylus' Seven Against Thebes.) The mothers of the heroes have brought the heroes' children to Athens-famous for hospitality to outcasts-to seek help from Theseus, king of Athens. They want him to force Thebes to surrender the bodies so they can be given a proper burial.

CHARACTERS

Aethra: Mother of Theseus, King of Athens.

Chorus: Mothers of the Argive heroes.

Theseus: King of Athens.

Adrastus: King of Argos, defeated in his attack on Thebes.

Herald: From Creon, King of Thebes.

Evadne: Wife of Capaneus, one of the seven heroes who marched against Thebes.

Iphis: Father of Evadne.

Children: Of slain heroes.

Athena: Goddess of war and of wisdom, preserver of the state, protecting deity of Athens.

Messenger: Guards, attendants, soldiers.

SETTING

Before the temple of Demeter at Eleusis. (Demeter was goddess of agriculture and of the fruits of the earth. Eleusis was northwest of Athens, on the coast, and famous for its religious celebrations.)

Aethra, mother of King Theseus, has come to the temple of Demeter with an offering. She discovers Adrastus there, Argive king who led the attack against Thebes, and the mothers and the children of the heroes killed in the battle. They want Theseus' help in burying the heroes' bodies, and Aethra sends a herald to Athens to summon him.

When Theseus arrives he questions Adrastus closely and learns that he married his two daughters to Tydeus and Polyneices after misunderstanding a prophecy, which he foolishly failed to confirm by other means. He was also warned by a seer not to attack Thebes, but listened instead to the advice of young men: Theseus says he showed more courage than discretion. Adrastus humbly admits his mistakes and begs for help. In a speech which argues that reason should control man's actions, Theseus says that lack of reason and excessive ambition (hubris) caused Adrastus' downfall; his conclusion is that he can see no justification for endangering Athens to help him. Adrastus says he came for help, not judgment, but submits to Theseus' decision.

The Chorus and Theseus' mother come to Adrastus' support. She points out that he might well be considered a coward if he refuses to help; she adds that he has an obligation to justice and to Hellenic standards. Persuaded by them, he decides to put the matter to a vote before the townspeople.

Comment

Theseus might have been a more interesting hero had he resisted the emotional appeal of his mother and remained the rigid logician, but this very inconsistency makes him more human. Besides, Euripides' patriotic propaganda would hardly have been served by rigid logic-Athens must be shown as just and generous.

After the citizens are consulted, a message is sent Creon declaring that, unless he permits the bodies to be buried, Theseus will attack. Before the message can be sent, a Theban Herald arrives and engages in an argument with Theseus on the virtues of despotism. Theseus defends democracy and rule by fixed laws. When the Herald declares that Creon will never surrender the bodies, Theseus prepares to attack.

Comment

The argument on the virtues of democracy would not only flatter an Athenian audience but would be relevant to the current political situation. In 421 B.C. Argos was considering a treaty with Boeotia, an enemy of Athens. This play calls attention to the fact that Athens and Argos have a common form of government, antipathetic to that of Boeotia (in which Thebes is located).

After a choral interlude, a messenger announces that Theseus has won the battle and could have taken the city, but has stopped his men outside the walls, declaring he came only for the bodies. He has given the soldiers a proper burial; the bodies of the slain heroes he has brought to Eleusis. Adrastus gives a eulogistic description of each hero, and the bodies are carried off-stage to the funeral pyre. Capaneus, one of the heroes, who had been killed by a bolt of lightning from Zeus while scaling the wall of Thebes, is burned separately as a consecrated corpse.

Comment

He had said only Zeus could keep him from scaling the walls. His defiance of Zeus in this statement brought his death. His fate is the classic example of hubris.

During the ceremony, Capaneus' wife, Evadne, appears on a high rock near his funeral pyre and throws herself into the flames. Her father, Iphis, who had lost a son in battle at Thebes, is thrown into despair by his daughter's violent death. In a bitter speech he bewails the lonesomeness of old age and denounces those who try to extend the span of life.

From the funeral pyre comes a procession of children carrying urns with the bones of their fathers in them.

Athena appears, enjoining Adrastus to swear that the Argives will never attack Athens; a memorial commemorating this oath is to be erected in Athens. The children of the heroes, Athena says, will one day sack the city of Thebes.

Comment

The appearance of Athena seems intended to conclude the play with a formal agreement, relating the events of the mythic past with those of Euripides' time. There may be some conflict with the earlier statement that Adrastus' war was foolish: Athena promises revenge to the sons of the slain heroes. It is just as well to note that there is some doubt among experts about what the play means.

THE PLAYS OF EURIPIDES

ION

BACKGROUND

Like three other plays by Euripides, *Alcestis, Iphigenia in Taurus*, and *Helen*, *Ion* is a tragi-comedy. It is thought to have had a great influence on the Greek New Comedy (see General Introduction: Comedy). For its melodramatic plot, Euripides uses a little-known story from traditional mythology, and changes much of that, thus making surprise and suspense part of the dramatic effect.

CHARACTERS

Hermes: Messenger of the gods; also god of eloquence, prudence, and cunning.

Ion: Son of Creusa and traditional founder of Ionia, an area on the west coast of Asia Minor.

Creusa: Daughter of Erechtheus, king of Athens.

Xuthus: Husband of Creusa. Tutor: Of Creusa.

Priestess: In Apollo's temple.

Athena: Goddess of war and of wisdom, preserver of the state, patroness of Athens.

Chorus: Handmaidens of Creusa.

Attendant

SETTING

In front of the temple of Apollo at Delphi.

Hermes appears in front of the temple and tells the past history of Ion: when Erechtheus was king of Athens, his daughter Creusa, was raped by Apollo and secretly bore a child in a cave. Lest the infant (Ion) be discovered and her shame made known, she abandoned it in the cave, leaving him in his cradle. In the cradle she left some jewelry. Apollo ordered Hermes to carry the child in its cradle to the temple in Delphi, where he was found and raised by the Priestess. Creusa later married Xuthus, but she and her husband were childless. They have now come to the shrine to pray for offspring. Apollo plans to give Ion to Xuthus, and to tell Xuthus that he is the father so that Ion can lay claim to the land which is his birthright: Ionia.

Comment

The parentage of Ion supplies one of the political motives in the play: it helps justify Athens' claim to sovereignty over Ionia.

Ion comes out of the temple to perform his part in the temple rituals, cleaning the vestibule. This done, the Chorus (handmaidens of Creusa), enter and sing with Ion in admiration of the decorations of the temple. The Chorus want to enter the inmost shrine, but Ion tells them this is forbidden until a sacrifice has been made. They are followed by Creusa, who came to inquire about her child; in talking of Ion, she pretends she is making inquiries for a friend seduced by Apollo. He warns her not to ask Apollo for information he may well wish to keep secret. Her husband, Xuthus, back from consulting another oracle, enters. He tells her he has been promised that they will not return home childless. Xuthus goes into the temple, Creusa to one of the outer shrines. Ion wonders about this woman who accuses the god of wrongdoing; he also wonders, how, if the stories are true, the gods can expect men to behave better than they do.

Comment

In many of his plays, Euripides expresses skepticism about the received mythology. The speech of Ion, above, indicates to some critics that Euripides intended this play as serious religious comment, attacking anthropomorphic religion.

The Chorus have no sooner finished their prayer to Athena that Xuthus' request for a child be answered than Xuthus rushes out of the temple and tries to kiss Ion. The oracle has told him that the first person he meets when he leaves the temple will be his son. He believes the oracle and assumes the boy is the consequence of a youthful indiscretion. He names the son "Ion"-"the first met". Ion wishes to know who his mother is, but Xuthus, in his joy, had not waited to hear this. Xuthus is anxious to depart immediately so Ion can claim his heritage in Athens, but Ion fears the jealousy of the Athenians and of Creusa; he wants to remain in the temple, where he has known happiness and peace. Xuthus says that his parentage can be kept secret for a time, so Ion agrees to go to Athens as a guest. The Chorus is sworn to secrecy.

The Chorus lament Xuthus' new-found son, foreseeing misfortune when Creusa discovers his identity. When Creusa returns, she brings her old Tutor. The Chorus tell her that Xuthus has a son now. The Tutor says Xuthus must have secretly had a son with another woman, had him raised in the temple, and is now trying to make her think Apollo is responsible. The Tutor recommends that she kill her husband and Ion; he offers to kill Ion himself at the welcoming feast. In her anger and unhappiness, Creusa addresses herself to Apollo, accusing him of treachery in allowing their son to die or disappear, and yet give a son to Xuthus. The Tutor and the Chorus are astonished to learn that Creusa had a child of her own. She retells her story to the Tutor and the Chorus. In indignation the Tutor recommends she burn down the shrine of Apollo and then kill her husband and Ion. She agrees only to killing Ion. She has two drops of blood from the Gorgon (a female monster with serpents for hair: Medusa); one drop can kill, the other heals. She gives the first drop to the Tutor to put in Ion's wine cup.

The Chorus approve of the murder; they say that if the poison doesn't work there is always the sword or strangling.

An attendant rules in to warn the Chorus that all has been discovered: during the banquet Ion had a premonition that something was wrong and ordered the guests to pour out their wine. A flock of pigeons descended to drink it from the ground, and the one drinking Ion's wine died. He accused the Tutor, who had filled the cups, and received a confession. Creusa rushes in, pursued by the Delphian elders, who had ordered her death. She takes sanctuary at the altar, but is about to be pulled away and killed by Ion when the Priestess enters. She brings Ion the cradle in which he was found and tells him it will enable him to find his mother. Creusa identifies the cradle; Ion is suspicious, but she tells him correctly what he will find inside. After they have joyfully embraced, Ion takes her aside and suggests that perhaps her story about Apollo was made up to hide some indiscretion. Just as Ion is about to consult the oracle, Athena appears. She says Apollo has not come himself lest indiscreet mention of his past be made. She confirms that Apollo was the father of Ion, but says that Xuthus is not to be told this. Ion will become King, and his children will found Ionia. Creusa and Xuthus will have two children, Dorus and Achaeus, who will father the Dorians and the Achaeans. Creusa is now reconciled to Apollo.

THE PLAYS OF EURIPIDES

IPHIGENIA IN TAURIS

BACKGROUND

Like three other plays by Euripides, *Alcestis*, *Ion*, and *Helen*, *Iphigenia in Tauris* is a tragi-comedy. The action is melodramatic, depending on romantic and sensational incidents, rather than character and development of serious subject matter. For this play Euripides drew upon a tradition that Iphigenia was not actually sacrificed at Aulis by Agamemnon (See Aeschylus, *Oresteia*, above), but was saved by Artemis and made a priestess in her temple.

CHARACTERS

Iphigenia: Daughter of Agamemnon.

Orestes: Son of Agamemnon.

Pylades: Friend of Orestes.

Thoas: King of the Taurians.

Athena: Goddess of war and of wisdom, preserver of the state.

Chorus: Captive Greek Women, attendant on Iphigenia in the temple.

Herdsman

Messenger

SETTING

Before the temple of Artemis in Tauris. A bloodstained altar is visible.

Iphigenia appears before the temple dressed as a priestess and tells how she comes to be there. When the Greek fleet on its way to Troy was becalmed at Aulis, the prophet Calchas reminded Agamemnon that he had once promised to give Artemis the most beautiful creation of the year; that year Iphigenia had been born. Odysseus got her away from home by telling Clytemnestra, her mother, she was to marry Achilles. As she was about to be sacrificed, Artemis snatched her away and substituted a deer. Conveyed through the air to Tauris, Iphigenia was made a priestess.

Comment

This version of the sacrifice of Iphigenia is often compared to Abraham's sacrifice of Isaac in Genesis. Both stories, in the history of religion, have served the etiological purpose of explaining the cessation of human sacrifices.

In Tauris, the fierce king Thoas has ordained that all fugitive Greeks be sacrificed in the temple. Iphigenia is to perform rites preliminary to the actual sacrifice. She is troubled because she has dreamed that she was home in Greece, and that an earthquake destroyed her father's house, leaving only one pillar. Over that pillar she performed the rites of Artemis, preliminary to a sacrifice. She interprets the dream to mean that Orestes, her brother, is dead.

Iphigenia goes into the temple, and Orestes and Pylades enter cautiously. Orestes, still pursued by the Furies for the murder of his mother, has been told by Apollo to steal the statute of Artemis from the Taurians and take it to Greece; this task is to end the Furies' pursuit. Pylades recommends that they wait until dark-they leave the stage to hide.

Iphigenia and the Chorus come out of the temple and lament the death of Orestes.

A Herdsman comes in to tell Iphigenia to prepare for a sacrifice: he and his companions had driven their cattle to the sea that morning to wash them and two Greek strangers were there. One of these strangers began raving about the Furies pursuing him. Believing the bulls to be Furies he set about killing them with his sword, and the herdsmen had stoned him. When he collapsed, the other warded off the stones until his friend's recovery; whereupon they both attacked their herdsmen, who scattered. Finally, the two fell exhausted and the herdsmen captured them. They were taken to King Thoas, who ordered them sacrificed.

After the herdsman departed, Iphigenia says that the two Greeks will find her relentless; she used to be gentle to those about to be sacrificed, but now that Orestes is dead, her heart is hardened. In a sudden burst of passion, she denounces human sacrifice, saying the Taurians, who love bloodshed, falsely accuse the goddess of desiring it. Gods are not evil, she says.

Comment

One of Euripides' favorite **themes** was attacking anthropomorphism (giving human characteristics to divine beings) in Greek mythology. Along with Plato, he added goodness to the mystery of deity.

The Chorus wonder why the two Greeks set sail, and how they managed to pass the dangerous rocks. They wish someone would come to free them from slavery and take them back to Greece.

Orestes and Pylades are brought in to Iphigenia to be prepared for the sacrifice. Iphigenia questions Orestes about Greece, and, although he does not reveal his identity, he tells her Orestes is still living. She offers to spare one of them if he will carry a letter to Greece. Orestes insists on being the one to die. While Iphigenia is in the temple writing the letter, Orestes and Pylades speculate about her identity: she would not have been so moved to hear of Greece had she no stake in its fortunes. Pylades refuses to let Orestes die alone; he is married to Electra (Orestes' sister) and would be accused of killing Orestes to get his estate. Orestes tells him to go back home and beget children to ensure the perpetuation of his line; he, for himself, is ready to die; such are the misfortunes bequeathed by Apollo, who has deceived and betrayed him.

When Iphigenia comes out of the temple, she reads the letter to Pylades lest it should be lost. It is addressed to Orestes;

Pylades delivers it immediately. After a happy scene of reunion, Iphigenia learns that Orestes has been sent by Apollo to steal the statue of Artemis. Iphigenia proposes a plan for their escape; she will claim that the two Greeks are polluted by bloodshed and must be cleansed in the sea. The statue, profaned by their presence, must likewise be cleansed in the sea. They will go near to the place where Orestes' ship is hidden and flee from there. Iphigenia promises to take the captive women of the chorus with her and they agree to remain silent.

The Chorus tell how they dislike serving Artemis and sing of their return home.

King Thoas approves Iphigenia's plan to cleanse the statue and the two Greeks. She orders that the townspeople be told to stay in their houses and that Thoas and his retinue cover their faces, so the sight of the strangers will not pollute them. Orestes and Pylades are put in chains and join a procession to the seashore. Iphigenia carries the statue of Artemis, and the Chorus sing a hymn to Apollo as they ceremoniously depart.

A messenger rushes in to tell the king that Iphigenia and the two strangers are trying to escape. There has been a fight near the boat, which has sailed, but, on reaching the harbor's mouth, been driven towards the rocks. If the king hurries and the wind does not change, he can probably capture them. Thoas commands his people to follow; he tells the captive women they will be punished when he returns.

Athena appears from above and tells Thoas not to pursue; the gods are with Orestes. She calls to Orestes at sea and tells him to return for the captive women. When he arrives in Greece he shall build a temple to the Taurian Artemis, where Iphigenia shall be the priestess. At the annual celebrations a little human blood is to be drawn in memory of the original savage rites.

Comment

With the words of Athena, Euripides celebrates the origin of the Taurian Artemis in Greece and explains the rites performed there. As etiology, the play explains the substitution of a symbolic act for actual human sacrifice.

THE PLAYS OF EURIPIDES

HELEN

BACKGROUND

Like three other plays by Euripides-*Alcestis, Iphigenia in Tauris,* and *Ion-Helen* is a tragi-comedy. The sympathy for Helen and the frivolous attitude toward the Trojan War are opposite to Euripides' attitude toward the same subjects in his tragedies.

CHARACTERS

Helen: Wife of King Menelaus.

Teucer: A Greek warrior who fought in the Trojan War.

Chorus: Captive Greek women, attendant on Helen.

Menelaus: King of Sparta.

Theoclymenus: King of Egypt.

Theonoe: Sister of Theoclymenus.

Portress

Servant

The Dioscuri: The deified heroes, Castor and Polydeuces, sons of Leda and Tyndareus, brothers of Helen.

SETTING

In front of the palace of King Theoclymenus in Egypt. The palace is near the mouth of the Nile. Nearby is the tomb of Proteus, the father of Theoclymenus.

Helen is seeking sanctuary at the tomb of Proteus from Proteus' son, Theoclymenus, now king of Egypt, who wants to marry her. Her explanation of events which led her to Egypt begins with the judgment of Paris-he had adjudicated Aphrodite more beautiful than Hera or Athena: Aphrodite had promised him the world's most beautiful woman if he would do so. Helen, Menelaus' wife, was this woman. Hera, furious that she had not won, substituted a phantom for Helen. The real Helen was carried by Hermes to stay with King Proteus of Egypt, whom Zeus believed to be the most virtuous man living. Proteus has died, and to avoid marrying his son, Helen is seeking sanctuary. She says that the Trojan War was instigated by Zeus to rid the world of excess population.

Comment

The version of Helen's life which Euripides uses in this play was apparently put forth by a cult which worshipped Helen some time previous to the fifth century; its adherents desired to free her name from the many disreputable charges which had grown up around it. Stesichorus, a sixth century B.C. poet, used this version.

Teucer, a Greek Warrior who fought at Troy, enters in search of the prophetess Theonoe. From him Helen learns that her mother Leda has committed suicide, that her brothers are dead, that the Trojan War has been over seven years, that the Greek fleet was scattered by a storm on its way home, and that Menelaus has been given up for dead. She does not reveal her true identity to Teucer, although he is astonished at her likeness to the Helen he saw at Troy, and whom he hates. Helen tells him to leave without seeking the prophetess, for the king of Egypt kills all Greek visitors.

The Chorus of captive Greek women enter and join Helen in lament over the bad news she has just received. Helen says she must have been born to be a monster to the world. Hadn't her mother Leda been seduced by Zeus in the form of a giant swan? Hadn't she been born enclosed in an egg? She has lost her good name although she has never sinned; she is an exile among barbarians, without husband and family; and, if she ever returns to Greece, she will be blamed for the sins of the phantom. She resolves to commit suicide. The Chorus advise her to consult the prophetess Theonoe to confirm the news Teucer brought before doing anything rash. Still blaming her beauty as the cause of her misfortunes, Helen goes into the palace with the Chorus.

Alone, and dressed in rags, Menelaus enters. His ship has been the sailors. He knocks at the palace gate to find out where he is, and the portress informs him that he'll be killed if the king hears wrecked; he and the phantom Helen have escaped with several of his presence. She also tells him that Helen (the true Helen) has lived there since before the Trojan War. Menelaus decides not to leave, believing his name sufficient to get him food. That there is a Helen living there he dismisses as a coincidence.

Theonoe has told Helen that Menelaus is alive and will arrive in Egypt at the end of his wandering. Discussing this with the Chorus as they come out of the palace, Helen sees Menelaus. They recognize one another, but Menelaus refuses to believe her story of the phantom. A messenger, who is an old servant of Menelaus, comes to tell Menelaus that Helen has ascended into the air laughing at the Greeks, who have fought the Trojan War for a phantom. He is relieved to see Helen in front to the palace, and tells her he didn't know she could fly. His words have confirmed Helen's story of the phantom, and she and her husband have a joyful reunion.

Menelaus sends the messenger back to tell the others what has happened; they are to wait on the beach until Menelaus shall have got Helen away from the palace. Helen says they don't have a chance of getting away without the connivance of Theonoe. If they fail to escape, they swear to die together. Theonoe comes out of the palace, already aware of Menelaus' presence there. She says that Hera has decided to let them get safely home, but Aphrodite is angry, fearing the Greeks will discover she bribed Paris with Helen to sway his judgment. Theonoe tells them that whether they get home or not is up to her, and, to protect herself, prepares to send a servant to tell the king of Menelaus' presence. But both Helen and Menelaus plead with her in the name of her illustrious father, and in the name of justice, to let them go, and she decides to tell her brother nothing. Urging them to pray to Aphrodite and Hera, she returns to the palace.

Helen proposes a scheme for their escape. She will pretend that Menelaus is a messenger who saw "Menelaus" die. She will go into mourning and ask for a ship, that the funeral may be held at sea. Menelaus' sailors will take command of the ship and everyone can return home in it.

The Chorus lament the many who died in the Trojan War for a phantom sent by Hera. How can mortals believe in or trust the gods?

King Theoclymenus comes in from hunting. He has heard that a Greek is in Egypt, and when he sees that Helen is not at the tomb believes that she has escaped. Then Helen comes out of the palace dressed in mourning, and she convinces Theoclymenus that Menelaus is dead. He grants the request for a funeral ship, and Menelaus is put in charge of the arrangements. Helen agrees to marry Theoclymenus as soon as the funeral is over.

The Chorus say that when the goddess Persephone was abducted by Hades, her mother, Demeter, was so unhappy that she caused all vegetation to die on earth. Zeus cured his mother's (Demeter's) unhappiness by sending the Muses to cheer her with music, and Demeter soon began to sing herself.

Comment

This highly irrelevant song of the Chorus is apparently intended to be no more than an entertaining interlude. They make no comment on the action, thus maintaining the suspense at a crucial point.

Helen, Menelaus, and Theoclymenus come out of the palace. All is arranged for the funeral: Menelaus is armed and the Egyptian sailors have been ordered to obey him. King Theoclymenus, thinking of his imminent marriage, goes into the palace. Menelaus prays to Zeus wor luck, and he leaves with Helen and their attendants for the ship.

The Chorus hope they have a speedy voyage and a happy return to Greece.

A messenger rushes in to tell Theoclymenus that Helen and Menelaus have escaped. The messenger had been on the boat, which took the shipwrecked companions of Menelaus to the funeral, and on a word from Menelaus, they took out swords and killed the Egyptian oarsmen. A few jumped overboard and swam to shore. Theoclymenus strides toward the palace, intent, because she betrayed him, on killing his sister. He is stopped by a servant, who tells him that it is King Theoclymenus who is in error. Theoclymenus is about to kill the servant, when the Dioscuri (Castor and Polydeuces) appear from above. They tell him that Helen's departure is according to the will of the gods. They say that Helen will get safely home and, after her death, will achieve fame as a goddess-as have they, the Dioscuri.

Comment

As is characteristic of a tragi-comedy, Helen has no tragic **theme**, nor does it put forward any serious intellectual argument. It mocks the gods, but does not attack religion. The misfortunes represented are pathetic but not tragic; the ending is relatively happy for everyone. The plot is melodramatic and kept lively to the very end, when Castor and Polydeuces appear, interesting in themselves and neatly ensuring the safety of Theonoe.

THE PLAYS OF EURIPIDES

TROJAN WOMEN

BACKGROUND

The Trojan Women is one of the best antiwar plays ever written. Treatment of its **theme**, however, was more than mere literary exercise for Euripides. Written in the midst of the Peloponnesian War (431-404 B.C.), and presented the year after Athens had captured the neutral island of Melos, killed all surviving men, and sold the women and children into slavery, *The Trojan Women* reflects Euripides, disillusionment with the idea of a just and noble Athenian democracy. The ruling faction which instigated the attack on Melos was still in power when the play was presented; was, in fact, about to embark on an attack against Sicily, where the entire Anthenian force was to be destroyed. Public sentiment at the time may explain why the tetralogy in which the play appeared received only second place in the competition of 415.

The first two plays of the tetralogy were Alexander and Palamedes; the fourth was a satyric drama, Sisyphus. These plays have not survived, but the stories they told and some of Euripides' attitudes are known. Alexander is concerned with the early life of Paris (also called Alexander). Before his birth, his mother, Queen Hecuba of Troy, dreamed that she had given birth to a firebrand whose flames destroyed the city. Paris was therefore left exposed so that he should die. Found and reared by shepherds, he grew up to win athletic contests held by his father King Priam in his "memory." After the victory he was recognized and accepted as a son by Priam, despite the dire warnings of his sister, the prophetess Cassandra, who said he would cause the destruction of Troy. (For more information about Cassandra see Aeschylus' Agamemnon, above.)

Palamedes tells of one of the Greek leaders who sailed to Troy, Palamedes. He revealed that Odysseus, another of the leaders, was pretending to be mad so he could stay home instead of going to war. In revenge, Odysseus planted a forged letter from Priam in Palamedes' tent. Accused of treachery, Palamedes was found guilty and stoned to death. Evidence indicates the play was favorable to Palamedes.

Nothing is known of Sisyphus, but it has been conjectured that, because satyr plays were satirical, and because Sisyphus was sometimes represented as the father of Odysseus, this play satirized Odysseus.

The Trojan Women takes place just after the successful stratagem of the Trojan Horse, through which, after ten years of siege, Troy finally fell to the Greeks.

CHARACTERS

Poseidon: God of the sea.

Athena: Goddess of war and wisdom, patroness of Athens.

Hecuba: Queen of Troy, wife of Priam, mother of Hector, Paris, and Cassandra. The Greek form of her name is Hekabe.

Cassandra: Prophetess doomed never to be believed. Daughter of Hecuba and Priam.

Andromache: Wife of Hector, a prince of Troy killed by Achilles.

Helen: Wife of King Menelaus of Sparta, carried off to Troy by Paris.

Talthybius: A herald of the Greeks.

Menelaus: King of Sparta, brother to Agamemnon, leader of the Greek forces.

Chorus: Captured Trojan women, young and old, married and single.

Soldiers

SETTING

The battlefield a few days after the fall of Troy. Behind are the partly destroyed walls of Troy. To the right and left are huts in which live the captive women set aside for the Greek leaders.

Prologue (1-121)

The god Poseidon appears before the walls. He declares that he and Apollo built Troy and he still feels affection for it. Its king lies unburied now, its gold is being carried to Greek ships, and its holy places defiled with blood. The Greek soldiers restlessly wait for a favorable wind. Now that the temples are abandoned, Poseidon is leaving the city, submitting to Hera, Zeus' wife, who favored the Greeks. He sympathizes with the women of Troy, who are being divided among the conquerors. He calls particular attention to Hecuba, the Queen of Troy, who lies before him in the dust, her sons and husband slain, her daughter Polyxenai recently sacrificed at the demand of Achilles' spirit (See Euripides, *Hecuba,* above), and her daughter Cassandra given to Agamemnon.

The goddess, Athena, enters. She favored the Greeks to win, but is angry because one of them has attempted to rape Cassandra while she clung to Athena's altar.

Comment

This kind of crime was thought to have brought about the many misfortunes which plagued the Greeks after the Trojan War—for example, the wanderings of Odysseus and the murder of Agamemnon.

To gain her revenge. Athena has asked that thunder and lightning, wind and hail, strike the ships. She wants Poseidon to make the seas wild. He promises that as soon as the last ship has left the land his full fury will strike.

Comment

The misfortunes of the Greeks following the Trojan War were well known to the audience. Euripides' prologue dramatizes their divine origin, giving a viewpoint which imbues the following scenes with great irony.

Hecuba, who has been sleeping on the ground, awakens. She laments her woes: no longer is she among the lords of Troy. City, wealth, social position, and most of her family have been lost-nothing is left to her but to endure. She gazes at the Greek ships and deplores the great disasters they brought, all for the sake of the evil Helen. She calls to the other women to come out and sing with her as they had in Troy-but different songs.

Parodos (122-236)

Singing alternate verses, Hecuba and the Chorus of Trojan women speak of the Greeks preparing to sail, of being separated from one another, of their slavery, and of the cities to which they may be taken.

First Episode 237-512

The Greek herald Talthybius enters; and tells the women that lots have been cast, and they have been assigned to various Greek leaders: Cassandra is to be Agamemnon's concubine; about Polyxena the herald is vague, saying only that she is "to watch Achilles' tomb"; Andromache, the widow of Hector, is to go to Neoptolemus, son of Achilles; Hecuba herself to Odysseus. She laments her fate because of Odysseus' reputation for lying and cruelty.

Talthybius has just ordered his men to bring out the women when he sees flames inside the hut. He believes the women are trying to avoid slavery by killing themselves, but Hecuba tells him that what he sees is only Cassandra's torch. Carrying a torch, Cassandra comes out of the hut. She sings to Hymen, the god of marriage, of her joy in being chosen for a king's bride: she compares her mother's weeping to her own joy and invites her mother to laugh and join her dance.

Comment

Cassandra's prophecies were regarded as mad ravings because it had been ordained she should not be believed. This reputation for a kind of insanity is borne out by the foregoing scene. The scene is also a fierce travesty of a marriage hymn-the torch was a symbol of Hymen. Her exultation gives dramatic emphasis in these desperate moments that no conventional lament could have effected.

Hecuba recalls her plans for Cassandra's marriage day-how different from the present! She takes the torch from her daughter, remarking that all her griefs have not changed her frenzies; she still lacks wisdom. The other women, she says, should answer Cassandra's bridal song with tears. Cassandra insists there will be joy in her marriage: the axe is waiting which shall kill her and Agamemnon, and lead eventually to matricide.

Comment

Cassandra here prophesies the fall of the house of Atreus. When Agamemnon arrives home with Cassandra, his wife, Clytemnestra, kills them both. Orestes, Agamemnon's son, then kills his mother. (See Aeschylus, *Oresteia*, above.)

Even now, Cassandra says, the Trojans are happier than the Greeks. Why did the Greeks die? For one woman's beauty-no one had attacked their towns. They died in a foreign land, many fathered children at home they had never seen, and their graves are unmourned. The Trojans, on the other hand, died gloriously defending their country; they fought near their homes and were buried on their own soil. War is an evil, but there is triumph for those who fight well for just causes. Only these who dies in sin have cause for lamentation.

Comment

The sin of the Greeks was hubris, excessive daring, going too far. As Poseidon and Athena made clear in the prologue, even those gods who favored the Greeks during the Trojan War have turned against them now. The episode with Cassandra is the first delineation of several Greek outrages told about in this play. Thus, while we see the Trojans suffering, we see the Greeks sinning: our sympathy is with the Trojans, our fear for the Greeks.

Talthybius has stood spellbound during Cassandra's frenzy; he now declares that she'd be punished if she weren't mad. He can't understand Agamemnon-he wouldn't want Cassandra! He bids her walk quietly by his side and lets Hecuba know that someone will come to take her to Odysseus. When Cassandra hears this she complains that Apollo has betrayed her-he had told her that Hecuba would die in Troy. Odysseus, she says, will not get home for ten years. After repeating her prophesies regarding Agamemnon, she tears off her prophetic wreaths, consoles herself that she will soon join her father, Priam, in death, and goes out with Talthybius. Hecuba falls to the ground, where she lies bewailing the futility of her life; her sons, the princes of Troy, have been killed; her husband murdered at the altar and his city sacked; her daughters forfeited to the Greeks; she herself will wear rags and grind flour.

First Stasimon (513-568)

The women of the Chorus sing of the golden Trojan horse, dragged into the city as a gift for Athena. The plain where the Greeks camped lay silent that night, and in Troy a celebration began to mark the end of the war. At night the Greeks came out of the horse and defeated the city.

Comment

None of the choral odes in this play comment on the action of the preceding **episode**. This is not because the women of the chorus are insensitive to the misfortunes of individuals, but because they are, in a way, protagonists. The individuals who appear in the separate **episodes** of the play do indeed suffer, but they represent only a part of the whole. The women of the chorus are preoccupied with the fall of an entire city; they call attention to a multiplicity of unfortunate fates.

Second Episode (569-800)

Andromache enters, carrying her child. She is riding on a chariot piled with loot and on its way to the Greeks. On arrival she will become the concubine of Neoptolemus, son of Achilles, her husband's killer. In a lament, she tells Hecuba of a new misfortune: Polyxena has been offered up as a sacrifice to Achilles' spirit. Andromache says the dead are better off than the living; they cannot know paid nor contemplate their mistakes. As for herself, her care in life has been to achieve a high reputation as Hector's wife, and now she must go to Neoptolemus' bed. Is not Polyxena better off? she asks Hecuba. Did she ever have to suffer so much?

Hecuba replies that she has never been on a ship, but has heard that the sailors face a storm until it becomes too strong; then they yield. Andromache must do the same, honoring her new lord and raising her child among his father's enemies; for someday Troy may be rebuilt. Talthybius returns and tells Andromache that the Greeks have ordered her son, Astyanax, killed; he is to be thrown from the walls of Troy. Odysseus has instigated the proceeding, saying that the son of Hector may be a danger to the greeks when grown to manhood. Andromache recalls the nights she watched over Astyanax' childhood sicknesses and then fiercely curses Helen as the cause of Troy's misfortunes. Talthybius gently and reluctantly takes the child from her and goes toward Troy. Andromache is set on the chariot again and driven toward the ships.

Comment

As becomes clear by the end of the second **episode**, there is no conventional "plot" developed in this play. The sequence of scenes, rather than being based on an order of events, contain an ever-increasing intensity of pathos. The structure of the play is episodic.

Second Stasimon (801-852)

The Chorus sing that this is not the first time Troy has been taken. Long ago, in the time of Priam's father, King Laomedon, Heracles and Telamon defeated the city. Yet the gods did not always hate Troy. Ganymede, the most handsome of boys, was a Trojan and was taken by Zeus to be his cupbearer. And Tithonus, a son of Laomedon, was loved by the goddess of the Morning, who carried him to the skies to be her husband.

Third Episode (853-1052)

King Menelaus enters, richly dressed and accompanied by a bodyguard. He declares that it is indeed a beautiful day on which he can get back the woman he fought for. Then he suddenly checks himself and says that he came to Troy not for her but for the thief who stole her-Paris, who is dead. Helen is now among the captive women, and the Greek leaders have given her to Menelaus to do with her what he will. He has decided not to kill her in Troy, but to carry her home and punish her. While the soldiers he sends to get her are gone, Hecuba praises the god who is bringing justice. She warns Menelaus not to be snared by Helen's beauty; it would be better if he were not to look at her.

Helen proudly comes from the hut and calmly asks whether she is to live or die. If she is to die, she wants only to be allowed to speak first. Menelaus does not want to hear her, but Hecuba asks not only that she be allowed to speak, but that she, Hecuba, be allowed to answer her. Helen, arguing for her life, adduces the history of Paris as the first point in her case. He should have been killed at birth because of the prophecy given his mother. When he judged Aphrodite more beautiful than Athena or Hera, Aphrodite fulfilled her promise to give him the most beautiful woman in the world, Helen. She is thus only a victim of the gods. When Paris came to visit Menelaus, he came with the goddess of love's assistance. Nor did it help matters for Menelaus to sail for Crete and leave them alone! Surely this was all Aphrodite's fault; Menelaus should punish her. Helen says she tried several times to lower herself from the Trojan walls after Paris was killed, but the Trojans always caught her and pulled her back.

Hecuba says that the story of Paris judging the goddesses is nonsense; and if Aphrodite was so anxious to help Paris, why did he have to take a ship? She could have wafted him there by simply willing it. What happened was simply that Helen saw a richly dressed and handsome man and fell in love with him. In Troy she always praised the side winning that day. And as for her escape attempts, Hecuba asks, why had she never heard of them before? Who caught her? Why did she refuse Hecuba's offers to lead her out of the city? Had Helen had any shame she would have committed suicide; she certainly wouldn't be appearing well groomed and proud now-she would be crawling.

Menelaus orders Helen to walk before him toward the Greeks; there are many there who long to stone her and she'll be dead by night. Helen kneels before him and embraces him; he weakens and tells the soldiers to escort her to the ship. Hecuba warns him that, a lover once, he will love again. He makes no promise on this score, but says he will sail on a different ship from Helen.

Third Stasimon (1053-1112)

The Chorus sing to Zeus, asking how he would have forgotten the many temples built and sacrifices offered up in the city of Troy. The men are dead and the women and children have been left to suffer; they hope death will come soon, and that, like the other captives, the proud Helen will never again see her homeland.

Exodos (1113-1324)

Talthybius comes back from Troy, carrying the dead body of Astyanax. Andromache has sailed with Neoptolemus already but has requested that her son be buried in the shield of his father, Hector, Talthybius leaves the body with Hecuba and goes out to dig the grave. Hecuba decries the fear that led the Greeks to kill the boy. She laments the youth and love he will never know, and remembers the nights he slept with her. The women of the Chorus join in her grief while she prepares the body for burial. Hecuba rises from her task and says that she has just had a vision of the hand of God, and that there was nothing in it but a rod of affliction; prayer and sacrifice are all in vain. She bids the women take the child's body to his grave. Talthybius returns and orders the soldiers to set fire to what remains of Troy. Hecuba tries to run into the flames and die with Troy, but the soldiers hold her back. Talthybius has said that the last ships are waiting-with a great crash the tower collapse, and the women are led away.

THE PLAYS OF EURIPIDES

ELECTRA

BACKGROUND

Electra dramatizes the same events as do Aeschylus' *Choephoroe* and Sophocles' *Electra.* Aeschylus' version was the second part of a trilogy which had profound religious significance. Euripides emphasizes the psychological states of his characters. In some respects, Euripides is "correcting" Aeschylus' moral view. Whether this play was written before or after Sophocles' version has never been established, since the evidence is slender and can often be used to argue either way. Current scholarship tends to think that Sophocles' *Electra* is the earlier play.

When King Agamemnon returned to his home in Argos after the end of the Trojan War, he brought with him as a concubine Cassandra, a Trojan princess. Clytemnestra, Agamemnon's wife, has taken Aegisthus as a lover during her husband's absence. The day Agamemnon returned, he was murdered by Clytemnestra and her lover (see Aeschylus' *Agamemnon*). *Electra* begins several years later.

CHARACTERS

Clytemnestra: Widow of King Agamemnon.

Electra: Daughter of Agamemnon and Clytemnestra.

Peasant: Husband of Electra.

Orestes: Brother of Electra.

Pylades: Friend of Orestes.

Chorus: Country women.

Old Man: Former servant of Agamemnon.

Messenger

The Dioscuri: Castor and Polydeuces, brothers of Clytemnestra and Helen; they joined the immortals after their death and appear in *Electra* as the deus ex machina.

SETTING

In front of the hut of the Peasant, located on the borders of Argolis, a peninsula in the northeast of the Peloponnesus.

The time is early morning.

THE PLAYS OF EURIPIDES

Prologue (1-166)

The Peasant, alone on the stage, delivers the prologue, a summary of the history of Agamemnon's family. He tells how Aegisthus married Clytemnestra after the two of them murdered Agamemnon; they now rule Argos. Orestes, Agamemnon's son, was sent away for safety by a friend of Agamemnon's to Phocis (about ninety miles north). Electra, Orestes' sister, was kept at home and all offers of marriage were refused for her by Aegisthus, who was afraid a son of hers might avenge Agamemnon. His fears reached such a pitch he finally decided to kill her, but her mother, Clytemnestra, managed to save her life by agreeing she marry the Peasant. (A low-born child could make no claim). Aegisthus also offered a reward to anyone who killed Orestes. The Peasant says his family is noble enough, but they are poor. Because he regards Electra to be far above his station, the Peasant has never consummated the marriage.

Comment

Electra's marriage to the Peasant is Euripides' innovation. In the usual version, she marries the friend of Orestes, Pylades. The change increases the pathos of Electra's situation as a victim of Aegisthus. She, like Orestes, is visibly excluded from her patrimony. Locating the play in the country rather than in front of the palace also gives greater **realism** to the necessarily cautious return of Orestes. The prologue also gives us the fact of Electra's virginity, something that is ever-present in Electra's mind, almost to the point of obsession. She is, remember, at least 25 years old.

Electra comes out of the hut, her head shaved and dressed in rags, carrying a water pitcher. She performs these menial tasks to remind the gods of Aegisthus' insults. Her husband hates to see so highborn a lady do such work, but she has great respect for his kindness and wants to help him as much as she can.

Comment

This scene helps to humanize the traditional representation of an Electra outrageously obsessed by revenge. However monstrous she may seem later as the accessory in her mother's murder, her kindness to her husband and her respect for his virtues remain as the first impression of her character.

It is, however, possible to give this scene a completely different interpretation, i.e., that Euripides here, as elsewhere in his plays, presents favorable initial appearance of a character in order to shock us all the more by his (unexpected) monstrous acts.

Electra goes to the spring and the Peasant to the fields. A moment later, Orestes and Pylades enter. They have come from Phocis to avenge Agamemnon's murder. The night before Orestes left a lock of his hair and made an offering on his father's tomb and is now seeking Electra. When he sees her returning with water, he thinks she is a servant and approaches to make inquiries. As Electra comes in, she sings of the death of Agamemnon, of the unknown fate of her brother, and of the cruelty of Clytemnestra and Aegisthus.

Comment

Aeschylus' version made Clytemnestra chiefly responsible for the death of Agamemnon; Euripides places the blame chiefly on

Aegisthus. Euripides also emphasizes much more the illicit love of Clytemnestra.

Parodos (167-212)

The Chorus of country women come in to tell Electra that all the women are expected to attend a sacrifice in Hera's temple in three days. Electra says she lives only for her misery; fine clothes and dancing are not for her. The women try to overcome her reluctance, but she can now live only like a wanderer, outcast by gods and men.

First Episode (212-431)

Orestes and Pylades approach the woman to the great alarm of Electra. Orestes, who has been listening to Electra and the Chorus, now realizes that the girl he earlier thought was a serving girl is actually his sister. Nevertheless he exercises caution and pretends to be someone else. Orestes says he has brought a message from her brother. He is alive and well and desires to know how she is faring. No longer alarmed, or shy about answering his questions, she tells of her chaste marriage. He learns that she is willing to help Orestes kill their mother with the same axe she used to kill their father. Electra compares her own poverty and isolation to the oriental splendor in which Clytemnestra lives. In the palace, the blood of Agamemnon still stains the wall, and Aegisthus rides in Agamemnon's chariot and carries his scepter. When drunk, he throws stones at Agamemnon's grave and taunts Electra with the absence of her brother. She too wonders why Orestes has not returned, and when the Peasant enters, he asks her whether her brother even knows the way his father died.

After Orestes meets the Peasant, he is invited into the hut. Amazed at the high praise Electra has given her husband, Orestes generalizes about the nature of virtue. Neither birth, wealth, poverty, nor skill in arms give a man nobility-only by their actions can men be judged.

Electra rather sharply rebukes her husband for inviting such aristocrats into their lowly hut, but he replies that if they have genuine nobility, they'll be content with what is offered. She orders him to have Agamemnon's foster father bring more food. He will want to see the strangers, too, for he had saved Orestes years before and will enjoy news of him.

First Stasimon (432-486)

The Chorus sing of Achilles, who went with Agamemnon to Troy. Hephaestus (god of fire) made the armor for Achilles, and it was carried to him by the Nereids (the 50 daughters of Nereus, one of whom was Thetis, mother of Achilles). The shield was brilliantly wrought gold; it dazzled the eyes of the enemy. Agamemnon, the leader of many warriors like Achilles, was murdered by Clytemnestra. May the gods punish her!

Comment

A characteristic feature of the late plays of Euripides is the irrelevance of the Chorus' remarks. The stasimon above makes no comment on either the action or the characters; only at the end is it awkwardly related to Clytemnestra. One explanation is that in a melodrama such as *Electra*, the audience is expected to interest itself in exciting action and flamboyant characters; there are no major ethical issues for the Chorus to comment on.

This is not social drama, either, as Euripides presents it, and the Chorus has no particular involvement in the action's outcome.

Another explanation for the Chorus' irrelevancy may lie in the fact that in his old age Euripides was attracted to some of the new trends in music. Whereas in Aeschylus' day the music was rigidly subservient to the words, some of Euripides' younger contemporaries were experimenting with new techniques of composition which allowed for greater freedom in the relationship between words and music, with the result that the words became less important. We know that Euripides wrote in this new manner because Aristophanes makes fun of him for this; we also know that Euripides wrote an introduction to a piece by Timotheus, one of the most famous of these avant-garde musicians. Thus, even though the scores for all of his plays have vanished (except possibly for part of *Orestes),* we can be fairly certain that in some of his plays (and *Electra* may be one of them) the Choral odes were considered more as musical interludes, to be enjoyed more for themselves alone, than as commentary on the dramatic action. For more information on Greek music, see the Oxford Classical Dictionary, entry Music.

Second Episode (487-698)

The Old Man, who had been Agamemnon's foster father, and who had taken Orestes to Phocis, enters, laden with food. Having stopped at Agamemnon's tomb and seen the hair and sacrifice there, he suggests that Orestes left them, for no one else would have been so reverent. Electra replies that such "clues" mean nothing: a man's hair would be different from hers. And why should her brave brother come by stealth? She also denies the Old Man's suggestions that Orestes could have left a footprint or might still have some article of clothing she would recognize.

Comment

The three signs mentioned by the Old Man were used in the equivalent recognition scene in Aeschylus' *Choephoroe* (II. 164-245). The scene here, in contrasting as it does with the scene in Aeschylus' play, is often taken as an overt criticism of the earlier playwright's treatment. But this may not be the case. The recognition scene with the lock of hair, the footprint, and the cloth may go back to yet an earlier telling of the story, the *Oresteia* by Stesichorus, a Greek poet of the sixth century B.C. It is possible, therefore, that Euripides here is using a traditional element of the story, but giving it a very realistic slant.

When Orestes and Pylades come out of the hut, the Old Man recognizes Orestes by a scar on his forehead, acquired as a child while chasing a fawn with Electra. Electra and Orestes embrace, and the Chorus say that now her turn has arrived for victory. Orestes asks whether he has any friends who can help. The Old Man tells him he will not only have to act alone, but that he'll never succeed if he tries to kill Aegisthus and Clytemnestra inside the palace. However, Aegisthus is preparing oxen for a sacrifice at his estate. There, Orestes will be invited to the feast and can kill him at the first opportunity. Aegisthus' slaves, the Old Man cynically comments, will support the victor in the fight.

Clytemnestra is not going to the feast for fear of the citizens' reproaches; she is hated for her crimes. Electra proposes that Clytemnestra be told Electra has a child, and when she comes to see her low-born grandson, they can strike.

Comment

Of the three Greek plays representing Orestes' revenge, the character of Orestes is weakest in Euripides' version. He delays inordinately long, presumably out of caution or fear, to reveal his identity; he leaves the planning of the murders to the Old Man and Electra. He is not a coward, however; he is irresolute, and this makes an effective contrast to the determination of his sister.

Note also that he plans the murder of Aegisthus and Clytemnestra not so much to avenge the death of Agamemnon as to claim the kingship for himself-a far less noble, if not more realistic, reason.

In a very dramatic trio (a rarity in Greek tragedy), Electra, Orestes, and the Old Man pray for good success to Zeus, Hera, and the spirit of Agamemnon. Electra reminds her brother that it is time to act. She warns him that if he fails to kill Aegisthus, she will commit suicide.

Second Stasimon (699-746)

The Chorus sing of a lamb with golden fleece that Pan brought to the flocks of Atreus; but his brother Thyestes stole the lamb, with the help of Atreus' unfaithful wife, and gained the throne. To punish men for such quarrels, Zeus reversed the course of nature: great heat and drought ensued. Such tales of punishment make men listen to the gods, yet Clytemnestra failed to listen when she killed her husband.

Third Episode (747-1146)

Loud cries are heard in the distance and Electra comes out of the hut. A messenger brings the news that Aegisthus is dead. After graciously welcoming Orestes and Pylades to his feast, he attached no significance to their refusal to purify themselves after they explained they had already done so. Orestes was invited to make the actual sacrifice of the bull, and Aegisthus examined the entrails for signs of the future. The unfavorable appearance of the entrails caused him to fear that Orestes was near and threatening. Orestes reassured him and called for a cleaver to finish the sacrifice. While Aegisthus examined the entrails further, Orestes killed him from behind with the cleaver, severing his spine. The Chorus and Electra joyfully celebrate the death of Aegisthus.

Orestes and Pylades are welcomed by Electra as they enter with the body of Aegisthus. Electra is reluctant to follow Orestes' suggestion that the body be exposed to the beasts of prey, but she stands above it and rehearses her grievances: even after marrying Clytemnestra he did not rule in his house; he made orphans of Agamemnon's children; he relied on wealth; and he had an effeminate beauty. She turns disdainfully away from the body, and Orestes has it carried into the hut so Clytemnestra will not see it.

Comment

Compare with Electra's comments on the value of wealth and character Iago's speech in *Othello* (Act III, scene iii): "Good name in man and woman, dear my lord, Is the immediate jewel of their souls. Who steals my purse steals trash; tis something, nothing."

When they see Clytemnestra approaching in her chariot, Orestes doubts that he can kill his mother; he says the oracle of Apollo was foolish in ordering him to murder. Electra encourages him, taunts him with unmanly timidity, tells him men can be no wiser than the gods. Orestes goes into the hut as Clytemnestra enters, surrounded by gorgeously dressed Trojan attendants, who she says are compensation for her lost daughter (Iphigenia).

Comment

In the remainder of this scene, although both mother and daughter argue their causes, they are remarkably subdued: Clytemnestra because she is genuinely remorseful and desires a reconciliation, Electra because she does not want her mother to leave before being lured into the hut.

Clytemnestra justifies her murder of Agamemnon by saying he had killed their daughter Iphigenia for an unworthy cause-the Trojan War. Why should her daughter have been sacrificed to get Menelaus' wife back? And when he returned from the war he brought back a second bride, his mistress Cassandra.

At the invitation of Clytemnestra, Electra voices her grievances: Clytemnestra, she says, is famous for her unfaithfulness-no sooner had Agamemnon departed than she was beautifying herself. She never wanted Agamemnon home. Besides, if her complaint is against Agamemnon, why are Electra and Orestes cut off from their patrimony? Clytemnestra promises to oppress her no longer; she goes inside the hut to perform the sacrifices for the infant. Electra says she'll make a fitting sacrifice indeed!

Comment

The rags of Electra make a strong contrast to the gorgeous equipage of Clytemnestra in this scene, emphasizing Electra's poverty. The quiet patience of Clytemnestra and her wistful remorse emphasize Euripides' view that Orestes and Electra were not justified in their murders-not that Aeschylus and Sophocles approved of matricide, but they give it more emotional justification.

Third Stasimon (1147-1237)

The Chorus say that misery is changing sides; now justice comes to Clytemnestra.

Exodos (1238-1359)

Cries are heard from Clytemnestra; Electra and Orestes come from the hut spattered with her blood. The bodies of both Clytemnestra and Aegisthus are brought out, and Orestes laments the punishment he will suffer for these murders. Electra too laments her misfortunes to come, and Orestes charges her with changing like the wind because it had been she who urged the deed.

From above, the Dioscuri (Castor and Polydeuces, immortalized brothers of Clytemnestra and Helen) appear ex machina. They say Clytemnestra has been justly punished but that they were wrong to kill her. They imply that Apollo was wrong to order her death, but declare they will not speak against the god. They reveal that Electra is to marry Pylades; Orestes is to go into exile and will be pursued by the Furies and driven mad. He is to go to the image of Athena in Athens; a trial will be held on Ares' Hill, the Areopagus, and the precedent will be established that if equal votes are given, the accused is acquitted.

The citizens are to bury Aegisthus. Menelaus and Helen are to bury Clytemnestra.

The Dioscuri also reveal that Helen was never at Troy; only a phantom was seduced by Paris. The real Helen was safely in Egypt (see *Euripides' Helen*). Orestes and Electra tenderly say farewell to one another, and the Dioscuri, before they vanish, warn against doing injustice.

Comment

Euripides' interest in the psychology of his characters and the violent actions represented have led many to call the play a melodrama. Since it was not an integral part of a trilogy, the exodos ties up loose ends by narrating what will happen, and the ending is, ultimately, happy. There is some criticism of Apollo and the institution of the oracle running throughout the play, but this is not developed systematically.

THE PLAYS OF EURIPIDES

ORESTES

BACKGROUND

Written about five years after his *Electra,* Euripides' *Orestes* treats the same story in a far different manner. Several scenes border on the comic; topical **allusion** is more apparent than tragic seriousness; the deus ex machina (see General Introduction) wrenches the action from its logical development. Yet the play knew great popularity in antiquity: individual scenes are highly effective; *Orestes* presents a fascinating study of madness; the incidents are original and exciting. Those who have written about the play are by no means in agreement about its merit.

CHARACTERS

Electra: Daughter of Agamemnon and Clytemnestra.

Orestes: Brother of Electra.

Pylades: Friend of Orestes.

Menelaus: Brother of Agamemnon, King of Argos.

Helen: Wife of Menelaus; sister of Clytemnestra.

Hermione: Daughter of Menelaus and Helen.

A Phrygian Eunuch: Attendant of Helen.

Apollo: God who urged Orestes to kill Clytemnestra.

Tyndareus: Father of Clytemnestra.

Chorus: Maidens of Argos.

Messenger: Former servant of Agamemnon.

SETTING

In front of the palace of King Menelaus in Argos. It is six days after the murder of Clytemnestra and Aegisthus. Electra is watching over the couch of Orestes, who is asleep. She recounts the terrible crimes committed by the family of Atreus: how Atreus killed his brother's children and served them to him for dinner; how Arteus' son Menelaus married Helen, who caused the Trojan War; how his other son, Agamemnon, was killed by his wife, Clytemnestra; how she was killed by her son, Orestes; and how her spirit sent the avenging Furies to plague Orestes, driving him insane.

Electra is now nursing Orestes through fits of weeping, fever, and violence. Argos has found the matricides-for Electra helped her brother-guilty and they will soon be sentenced to die by stoning or by the sword. Their only hope is Menelaus, who is just arriving from Troy.

Helen has been sent to Electra's palace to await darkness before going home lest those whose sons were killed in the war stone her. She comes out of the palace to ask Electra to take an offering to the tomb of Clytemnestra, Helen's sister. Electra refuses to go near the tomb and suggests she send her daughter, Hermione. After Helen and Hermione leave, Electra says Helen has been a curse to the world; she notes that, for the offering to Clytemnestra, Helen cut off only the ends of her hair. She must be as vain and selfish as ever.

The Chorus of Argive women enter softly, to avoid awakening the sleeping Orestes. They sympathize with Orestes and make anxious inquiries; Electra urges them to speak more quietly-he has not eaten for six days and is very ill. She blames Apollo for their troubles, calling him an evil god.

Orestes awakens, much refreshed by his long sleep. Electra tells him Menelaus is near, and when he hears that Helen is already there, his thoughts turn to Helen's sister, his mother Clytemnestra, and a raving fit descends upon him. He sees the Furies attacking and calls for his bow. When the fit passes, he apologizes to Electra; he regrets having killed his mother, blaming Apollo for offering words but no real help. He urges Electra to rest, and lies down again himself.

The Chorus pray to the Furies and to Zeus that Orestes will be relieved from his suffering.

Menelaus enters, finds Orestes, and is shocked at his condition. He learns that Apollo has not stood behind Orestes. He is ostracized by the Argives and his sentence is about to be passed. While Orestes is begging Menelaus for assistance, Tyndareus, father of Helen and Clytemnestra, enters. He speaks violently against Orestes, saying he should not have taken the law into his own hands; but he does not approve of Clytemnestra or of Helen either. He urges Menelaus not to interfere in the citizens' decision. Orestes argues that Clytemnestra's lust for her lover Aegisthus alone led her to kill her husband; her murder was a public service, a warning to other wives. If anyone is to blame it is the father who began her, or Apollo, who ordered her death. Find Apollo and punish him! Tyndareus leaves to urge the citizens to stone Orestes and Electra; he again warns Menelaus not to interfere. Menelaus is undecided whether or not to help. Orestes argues that Menelaus owes a debt to Agamemnon that helping can discharge: did not Agamemnon lead the Greek forces because of Menelaus' grievance? Did not Agamemnon sacrifice his daughter Iphigenia to help the Greek ships? Menelaus says he will try persuasion with the citizens. More than that he cannot do, for he has been long at sea and has few friends or allies left. He leaves, and Orestes declares he has been betrayed; Menelaus can lead an army only in a woman's cause!

Orestes' friend Pylades comes in and says that his father has banished him for helping Orestes kill Clytemnestra. The streets are filled with armed men, and they realize that an attempt to escape would be useless. Orestes decides to appear at the trial determining his sentence to argue his case. They first go to pray at the tomb of Agamemnon. The Chorus sing of the woes of the house of Atreus, especially of Clytemnestra's murder and Orestes' madness.

A Messenger comes from the court and tells Electra that the case is lost-they were defended by only a single yeoman. Orestes has told the court they will both kill themselves and this has been accepted. Electra chants a history of her family's misfortunes and bewails her fate.

When Orestes and Pylades return, Electra learns that Menelaus was not present at the trial. Pylades plans to die with them, and suggests that first they get revenge on Menelaus by killing Helen. He points out that all Greece will honor them for killing the woman who caused so many deaths. Furthermore, is it fair that the house of Menelaus should prosper, while the house of Agamemnon is destroyed? Electra suggests they hold Hermione as a hostage, to protect themselves after Helen's death. If Menelaus will still not help them, they can slay Hermione too. They pray to Agamemnon for help; Orestes and his friend go inside while Electra waits for Hermione. A cry comes from Helen that she is being murdered; Electra calls encouragement to her brother and Pylades. When Hermione returns, Electra guides her into the house, where Orestes and Pylades hold her. The Chorus are happy that Helen has finally received justice.

A eunuch, terrified, comes out of the house. His hysterical report, after dealing with his own fear and some description of Helen's oriental manners, reveals that, as Helen was about to be slain, she vanished. Orestes comes out looking for Helen and bent on stopping the cries of the eunuch. The Chorus, while wondering whether to call for help or not, see flames coming from the palace; torches have been lighted to set it afire. Menelaus and his attendants enter. Orestes and Pylades appear on the roof of the palace, holding Hermione. Even though the life of his daughter is threatened, Menelaus will not risk his kingship by trying to defend Orestes. As Orestes orders his companions to set fire to his ancestral home, Apollo appears, holding Helen. Apollo says that he saved Helen, for she is to become immortal, along with her brothers, Castor and Polydeuces. Helen, in causing the Trojan War, was the instrument of the gods; but its means they achieved their purpose of reducing the surplus population. Orestes is to go into exile for a year, then return to Athens and be tried on the hill of Ares, where he will be found not guilty. He is then to marry Hermione. Electra is to marry Pylades. Orestes is to rule Argos, Menelaus to rule Sparta. Apollo will reconcile the citizens to Orestes. Everyone is happy with his fate, and Orestes apologizes for the hard words he spoke against Apollo earlier.

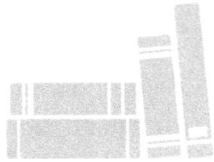

THE PLAYS OF EURIPIDES

PHOENISSAE

BACKGROUND

Phoenissae was one of Euripides' most popular plays among the ancients. The play is unique for its large cast and the range and sweep of its incidents. Euripides has altered the usual version of the story of *Oedipus* by having Jocasta still alive, and Oedipus still in Thebes, when their sons are killed.

CHARACTERS

Oedipus: Former King of Thebes.

Jocasta: Oedipus' mother and wife.

Eteocles: Now king of Thebes, son of Oedipus.

Polyneices: Brother of Eteocles, exiled.

Antigone: Daughter of Oedipus.

Creon: Brother of Jocasta.

Menoeceus: Son of Creon.

Teiresias: A blind prophet.

Chorus: Phoenician maidens.

Servant: Attendant on Antigone.

Messengers

Daughter Of Teiresias

Guards

SETTING

In front of the royal palace in Thebes.

Jocasta comes out of the palace alone and laments the day Cadmus founded Thebes: from him sprang Laius, Jocasta's husband, who sought aid from Apollo's oracle because he was childless. The oracle warned him to remain childless, for his child would kill him. He had a child, nevertheless, after going to Jocasta while drunk, and when the child was born, he told a shepherd to pierce the child's ankles with thongs, tie them, and leave him outside to die. (Oedipus means "he of the swollen ankles.") He was found by a shepherd and taken to Corinth, whose king, Polybus, raised him as a son. When grown, Oedipus suspected that Polybus was not his father and went to consult the Delphic Oracle. On the way he met Laius going to Corinth and was told to get out of the road. He refused. A fight ensued and Oedipus killed Laius. After Laius' death, the Sphinx brought plagues on Thebes; relief would come only when the riddle of the Sphinx was answered.

Comment

The riddle: What walks on four legs in the morning, two legs at noon, and three legs in the evening? Answer: Man, who crawls as a child, walks upright as an adult, and uses a cane in his old age.

Creon offered Jocasta as a bride to anyone who answered the riddle. By chance, Oedipus answered it and married his own mother, They had two sons, Eteocles and Polyneices, and two daughters, Ismene and Antigone. When Oedipus discovered Jocasta was his mother he blinded himself. His sons kept him confined within the house after they grew up, hoping all would be forgotten. Oedipus, unhinged by his misfortunes, delivered a curse on his sons, saying they would have to fight one another before they could share the inheritance of Thebes. They decided to share the throne in alternate years. Eteocles was first but refused to give up the throne after a year. Polyneices then married the daughter of King Adrastus of Thebes, and with his help has come to attack Thebes.

Comment

The attack on Thebes is the subject of Aeschylus' Seven Against Thebes. The aftermath of the defeat of Adrastus is the subject of Euripides' *Suppliants*. The stories of Oedipus are also the source of Sophocles' *Oedipus Rex, Oedipus at Colonus,* and *Antigone.*

Jocasta says she has arranged a truce so the brothers can meet and, she hopes, settle their differences without bloodshed. When Jocasta goes back into the palace, her daughter Antigone and an old servant appear on the roof. He points out to her the seven leaders of the attacking army; her brother Polyneices is among them.

The Chorus of Phoenician women enter. They had stopped in Thebes on their way to Delphi, where they are to serve in Apollo's temple. The impending war frightens them, especially knowing, as they do, that Polyneices has justice on his side.

Comment

The Chorus of this play are unusual insofar as they are strangers to the city; they thus serve as admirably objective commentators on the action.

Polyneices enters carefully, afraid of treachery. The Phoenician women receive him with obvious pleasure, and call Jocasta. She greets him warmly, and, at the same time, berates him for marrying a foreigner. Polyneices is deeply moved to see his own city again and inquires about his father and sisters. Jocasta questions him about the exile's life, and he says the worst part is not being able to speak his mind; he is also avoided by old friends, who forget the unfortunate and the poor.

Eteocles enters and Jocasta asks them to face one another and remember the purpose of the truce. Polyneices speaks first, pointing out that he kept his part of the bargain by leaving the city for a year; he will withdraw the attacking army only if he receives his original rights. Eteocles says that he subscribes to a different idea of honor and wisdom. He would do anything to keep his throne; in any other cause, virtue would be his aim. Polyneices can have half the property but not the throne; he is dishonoring Thebes by coming with an Argive army.

Jocasta tells Eteocles that Ambition is the worst of deities; only equality can bring peace among men. She asks Polyneices how he can face the gods if he defeats Thebes, and how he can face the Argives if he loses. The brothers will not be reconciled and agree to fight one another face to face.

The Chorus sing of Thebes, birthplace of Dionysus, founded by Cadmus, who killed Ares' dragon and reaped an army by planting its teeth. They call on the gods to help Thebes.

Creon comes in to discuss the strategy they are to use against the superior numbers of the enemy. Eteocles wants to rush out of the city and attack immediately. Creon has heard that each of the seven attacking leaders will concentrate on one of the seven gates of Thebes. He recommends that Eteocles assign a leader to defend each gate. Before going out to assign the troops, Eteocles tells Cteon that, should he be killed, Antigone is to marry Creon's son, Haemon, and Polyneices is not to be buried in Theban soil. While Eteocles arms, Creon is to consult Teiresias to see what heaven wills.

The Chorus sing of the difference between the terrible god of war and the charming Dionysus. They lament the survival of Oedipus the Sphinx' tricks, and the unnatural marriage of Oedipus.

The blind prophet Teiresias is led in by his daughter. He predicts that Eteocles and Polyneices will kill each other. He is reluctant to say what will save the city, but Creon urges him to tell. Menoeceus, Creon's son, must be sacrificed: Ares demands the blood in revenge for Cadmus' slaying of the dragon many years before. Teiresias goes off, grumbling about the hard life of a prophet, for he is always held responsible for the bad news he only foretells.

Creon tells Menoeceus to flee the city because Teiresias will tell the Theban leaders what he has predicted, and they will demand his death; Menoeceus pretends to agree, and Creon leaves. Menoeceus tells the Chorus that he will kill himself at the site of the dragon's den, as Teiresias has said he must to save Thebes.

The Chorus sing of the Sphinx, half maiden, half monster, that used to take youthful victims from the city until Oedipus came, a man both blessing and curse. They praise Menoeceus.

A messenger tells Jocasta that Menoeceus has killed himself, and that, following his death, there has been a great attack on the walls. Capaneus was struck by a bolt of lightning from Zeus, and Adrastus withdrew his forces. Jocasta's two sons are alive, but they have decided to settle the issue by single combat. Jocasta and Antigone rush to the battlefield, hoping to stop them.

The Chorus lament the fight between the brothers; they wonder which one they will have to mourn.

Creon comes in, followed by attendants carrying the body of Menoeceus. While he looks for Jocasta to prepare the body, a messenger arrives with the news that Polyneices and Eteocles have killed each other. Jocasta and Antigone arrived just after the fight but in time to hear the dying Polyneices' wish to be buried in Thebes. Picking up one of the swords, Jocasta killed herself. Quarreling then began as to who, with both champions dead, had won the day; the Thebans, who by chance had worn their armor to watch the single combat, soon settled the matter by attacking the Argives and, before they could arm, defeating them.

Antigone enters, followed by attendants carrying the bodies of her mother and brothers. She calls for Oedipus to come out of the palace and hear of the new sorrows he must bear. She tells him of the deaths. Creon claims that Eteocles left the throne to him. His first act is to banish Oedipus, for Teiresias has said Thebes would never prosper while he lives there. Creon also rules that Polyneices' body is to be thrown beyond the town limits for the birds and dogs to eat; anyone who tries to bury him will be executed. Antigone swears to bury Polyneices; she refuses to marry Haemon, and she plans to go into exile, leading her blind father. Oedipus touches the bodies of his mother and his sons; he tells Antigone that the wanderings foretold for him by the oracle are now beginning, and that he will die in Athens. Antigone says she will secretly bury Polyneices. With Antigone leading, they depart.

THE PLAYS OF EURIPIDES

BACCHAE

BACKGROUND

After Euripides' death in 407 in Macedonia three plays were found among his papers: the *Bacchae, Alcmaeon at Corinth* (which has disappeared), and *Iphigenia at Aulis* (which was never finished). An ancient commentator (scholiast) on the *Frogs* of Aristophanes tells us that these three plays were produced soon afterwards by his son, perhaps also named Euripides. They won first prize. Dionysus' coming to Greece from Asia or Thrace was a frequent **theme** in Greek poetry and art, and a number of lost plays dealt with the subject (including several by Aeschylus, and possible one by Sophocles). Dionysus also appears in the *Frogs* of Aristophanes. The *Bacchae* was widely read, admired, and quoted by classical Latin writers; though it has been much admired in modern times, it has not been adapted into new plays, as so many other Greek tragedies have been.

Dionysus (also called Bacchus, Iacchus, and Bromius by the Greeks, and later identified by the Romans with their own god, Liber) was the spirit of growth in trees and fruit; later he became associated especially with the grape vine and wine. Some festivals celebrating Dionysus become wild and orgiastic; he may be taken as a symbol of the intoxicating power of nature. Because Greek tragedy originated in the dithyrambic choruses of the festivals held in Dionysus' honor, he became the patron of tragic drama (Dionysus himself is called Dithyrambos at 1. 526, and elsewhere in Greek literature). The *Bacchae* dramatizes the establishment of Dionysus and his cult in Greece, as well as the effects of the cult and the attitudes of its detractors. Thus this play, which in **theme** is similar to *Hippolytus,* must have had an especially strong effect on its Greek audience. For here was a tragedy dedicated, as were all Greek plays, to Dionysus in which there were choral odes and dances specifically in his honor.

King Cadmus, who founded Thebes, had a daughter, Semele, loved by Zeus. According to a late version of the story, she was tricked by the jealous Hera, Zeus' wife, into asking Zeus to appear before her in the same form in which he appeared before Hera. Zeus had promised earlier to grant Semele a wish, and so he reluctantly appeared as the god of thunder. The lightning which accompanied him killed her. (This part of the story is told in the Handel-Congreve oratorio Semele.) She was prematurely delivered of a child by Zeus whom she was carrying. Zeus sewed the child into his thigh, thus preserving him until maturity. The child was Dionysus. In his travels he taught the cultivation of the vine.

CHARACTERS

Dionysus: God of the vine, son of Zeus and the Theban princess Semele (and therefore first cousin of Pentheus); has arrived in Greece to spread his worship; he delivers the prologue.

Cadmus: Former king of Thebes, father of Semele, grandfather of Pentheus.

Pentheus: The very young grandson of Cadmus, now king of Thebes; opposed to Dionysus and all that he stands for.

Agave: Daughter of Cadmus, mother of Pentheus.

Teiresias: An aged prophet of Thebes, who also appears in Euripides' *Phoenissae* and Sophocles' *Oedipus Rex* and *Antigone*.

Chorus: The Bacchae of the title (also called Maenads and Bacchantes), followers of Dionysus who have come with him from the East.

Soldiers

Messengers

SETTING

Before the castle of Pentheus, king of Thebes. Nearby is the sacred tomb of Semele.

Prologue (1-63)

The god Dionysus announces that he has come to Thebes, where his mother was killed, in the form of a man. He has seen his mother's tomb, where fire ignited at the time of his mother's death still smoulders, and he approves of Cadmus making a sanctuary there. His purpose is to call Greece to his worship, for despite his success in the East, from which he has just come, the Greeks are nonbelievers. Some, including Semele's sisters, even call Semele a wanton who claimed Zeus was the father of her child to hide her shame; they say the lightning was Zeus' punishment. To teach the nonbelievers a lesson, Dionysus has sent his spirit upon the women of the town; they have left their homes and run to the mountain sides in ecstatic frenzy. He is especially angry with King Pentheus, an outspoken skeptic; he and his people must be taught the god's power. Should the townspeople attack the worshippers who have come with him, he will appear as a god and lead his army against them.

Comment

Unlike the god whose speech opens *Hippolytus,* Dionysus does not reveal the action of the play. He makes clear, however, that Pentheus must make a decision, and that punishment for making the wrong decision will be severe.

Parodos (64-169)

The Chorus, devotees of Dionysus, enter. They wear the "uniform" of the cult: a fawn skin over white robes. Many carry the thyrsus, a staff with a pine cone on the end; their heads are decked with ivy. Some carry musical instruments. They praise Dionysus joyfully, telling of his birth, and calling to others to join them.

Comment

This parodos has one of the longest series of choral lyrics in Euripides' plays, and in structure and **theme** closely resembles the entrance hymn of the most early dramas, i.e., it is a ritual hymn to a god. Here, and elsewhere in the play, the Chorus reverts to the older, Aeschylean dramatic structure. The Chorus has an integral part in the plot and sings lengthy lyrics, both rare in the "typical" Euripidean play. This, of course, adds a greater feeling of unity to the play.

Note the thematic emphasis of this ode on Semele and the idea of birth, and how apt this is in a hymn to Dionysus, the spirit of growth.

First Episode (170-369)

The aged prophet Teiresias enters, wearing the garb of the Dionysian cult. He has come to celebrate the rites with the retired King Cadmus. Both are conscious of their great age and feeble condition, especially inappropriate to the rather energetic Dionysian rites, but both feel rejuvenated looking forward to the ceremonies. They are the only two men in Thebes preparing for the rites, but both agree that no god's worship should be ignored, even if old men have to attend wild dances.

Comment

While both old men accept Dionysus' godhead, they do not do so with the same irrational abandon as the Bacchae, who "become one" with Dionysus. Cadmus likes Dionysus, it seems, mostly because his divinity adds stature to Cadmus' whole family. Teiresias, a dramatic equivalent to the intellectuals of Euripides' own time (including Euripides himself), acknowledges Dionysus only after he has rationalized him according to late fifth century practices. Thus, at 1. 274 sqq., he says that Dionysus is the personification of wine (1. 284, "He, a god, is poured out to the gods"). And again (11. 285-297), Teiresias rationalizes Dionysus' birth by saying that, in order to fool Hera, Zeus broke off a piece (meros) of the atmosphere in the shape of the young Dionysus and gave it to Hera to hold as a hostage (homeros).

King Pentheus approaches and they draw to one side. Pentheus is furious about the new religion. He has heard that all the women have gone to the mountain sides to worship, taking wine jars with them and occasionally stealing into the woods where they enjoy love that is not of a god. He has imprisoned all his men could find, and he intends to stamp out the cult. He has also heard of a foreigner (actually Dionysus as a mortal) who is with the women, and threatens to kill him. When he sees his grandfather and Teiresias in the Bacchic garb, he accuses Teiresias of encouraging the religion for profit.

Comment

Pentheus is obsessed with the idea, which never leaves him, that the cult indulges chiefly in sexual immorality.

In defense, Teiresias argues that Dionysus is second only to Demeter, the Earth goddess, for blessings given to man. Demeter supplies the food he eats, and Dionysus supplies, in his liquid shower of wine, sleep, forgetfulness, and relief from grief. He praises frenzy, for it leads to prophecy, and he denies immorality in the new religion: that comes from the heart of the individual. He believes that Pentheus must be mad to war with a god.

Cadmus appeals to Pentheus' family pride: how marvelous to have a god spring from Semele! He urges him to worship even without believing. He reminds him of the way Actaeon was torn to pieces by his own hounds because he spurned Artemis.

Comment

Cadmus' belief is clearly not wholehearted. He is motivated by fear, family pride, and political shrewdness rather than faith.

Pentheus orders his men to destroy the rock seat where the ceremonies are held, and to find the effeminate-looking stranger who is leading them. Teiresias warns Pentheus against arrogance, and the two old men, supporting one another, go off to worship Dionysus. There they will pray that Pentheus not be punished, the city not destroyed.

Comment

Pentheus' decision to combat Dionysus' cult, the audience knows, will incur the god's wrath. The parting words of Teiresias show that the wrath might be expected as the natural consequence of ignoring any god. The Athenians, after all, had an altar dedicated to the "unknown god" in case their pantheon had any inadvertent omissions. Paul criticized the Athenians for this, Acts, 17:23.

First Stasimon (370-443)

The Chorus echo the fears of Teiresias. They invoke the goddess Holiness (Hosia in Greek) to behold Pentheus' scorn and hatred of Dionysus and all that he stands for. They typify Pentheus as someone who is clever without wisdom. Calamity comes to those who disdain mysteries they cannot see; mortality is so brief that it should not dare too much. The second part of the choral song expresses the Chorus' desire to escape to lands friendlier to Dionysiac revels. They praise Dionysus as a lover of peace and banquets, but a hater of all who scoff him.

Comment

The Greeks frequently personified abstractions, such as Dream (*Iliad*, Bk. II), Chance (who became very popular in Hellenistic times), Justice, etc. These divinities, just like Dionysus, represented natural, powerful, and (most important from the point of view of the Bacchae) undeniable forces that exist in the world. You couldn't disbelieve in Holiness any more than you could in holiness. Similarly, you can not disbelieve in Dionysus without denying that things grow.

The Chorus' comment that cleverness is not wisdom was a common Greek thought. Heraclitus, an earlier Greek philosopher, had said "You can know many things and still be a dummy," and the same thought is found in Plato's dialogue *Charmides*.

Second Episode (434-518)

The Soldiers enter with Dionysus, disguised as a human worshipper, and Pentheus comes out of the palace. One of the soldiers reports that Dionysus surrendered with so charming a grace that he had to apologize for arresting him. He also reports that the prison doors opened of their own accord and the worshippers captured earlier have returned to the mountain sides. Pentheus taunts Dionysus about his fair skin and long curls, and tries unsuccessfully to find out secret details of the Dionysian rites. Despite the warnings of Dionysus that sacred objects are being profaned, Pentheus has some of Dionysus' hair cut off, takes his thyrsus, and has him bound. Ordered imprisoned, Dionysus says he can release himself whenever he chooses. Pentheus takes the Dionysian maidens of the Chorus as slaves to work in his house or be sold. Dionysus again warns him he will pay for denying a god.

Comment

It would be difficult to point out a more effective dramatization of the sin of hubris than Pentheus' refusal to accept the miracles of the never-dying fire as Semele's tomb and the freeing of the women from prison. Euripides' careful preparation in the earlier scenes gives this superb encounter its effectiveness.

Earlier in this century, some critics denied that the stranger arrested by Pentheus was Dionysus. Such an interpretation loses all of **irony** present in the scene, e.g., ll. 500 f.: "And where is he? He is not visible to my eyes" says Pentheus, to which Dionysus replies "He is where I am."

Second Stasimon (519-575)

The Chorus sing of their trials and call Dionysus to help them. Their appeal is answered by the voice of Dionysus offstage, there is an earthquake; fire leaps up at the tomb of Semele; and maidens cast themselves on the ground.

Comment

This choral ode is an integral part of the action of the play. The anguish expressed stems naturally from the previous scene, and their prayer is answered by the miracles in front of the palace. The mood of this ode is similar to that of some of the Psalms (e.g., no. 7).

The earthquake was probably represented by a few stones falling from the palace, accompanied by noise made off stage.

Third Episode (576-861)

Dionysus, unbound, comes out of the place alone. Inside, he says, Pentheus has been sent visions: he has seen a bull ready for the offering and bound it, then run about for water when the flame rose above Semele's tomb, then stabbed an image of Dionysus in the prison-and finally fell exhausted.

Dionysus hears footsteps in the hall, and Pentheus emerges, unchastened: he orders the guards to bar the gates. Before his order is carried out, a panting messenger arrives from the mountain, where he has seen the townswomen. At dawn he saw three groups, one led by Pentheus' mother, Agave, sleeping on the mountainside-and no evidence of wine, music, and love-making, as Pentheus had expected. When they awoke they dressed in fawn skins belted with live snakes; food and drink sprang miraculously from rocks and the ground. Shepherds seeing them decided to capture Agave to gain the king's favor. When she passed by them in the ceremony, they tried to catch her, but she called to others, who chased the men and then attacked the cattle, tearing them apart and throwing the pieces around until the trees dripped blood. Then they destroyed a village, and the spears of the townspeople did not affect them. The messenger recommends that Pentheus accept the new god. In a rage, Pentheus calls his soldiers together to attack the women. Dionysus warns him not to-even offering to bring the women to the palace. Pentheus suspects a trick and sets off to attack them.

Comment

Pentheus' opposition to Dionysus and the new religion has grown as the play progresses. The more evidence he sees of divine origin, the more devoted he becomes to his original error. Yet he is no melodramatic villain. He is normally, as Cadmus says later, a well-meaning man, but he lacks imagination and, of course, humility.

With the same mildness that has marked his appearance throughout the play, which is physically represented by an appearance Pentheus called effeminate, Dionysus asks Pentheus if he would like to watch the women at their worship.

Comment

At this point begins the revenge of Dionysus. The prologue led us to expect a battle, but now a new tactic appears. Dionysus has remembered the great curiosity Pentheus showed earlier about the women's rights, and though no one need go so far as to call Pentheus a voyeur, one might detect prurience behind his upright facade.

Pentheus will have to dress as a woman for Dionysus to protect him from the worshippers, and only after much indecision about such a disguise, does he decide to go. He is reassured by Dionysus that he can get through the streets unseen. While Pentheus is in the palace dressing, Dionysus assures the Chorus that Pentheus will now be punished. Praying, he asks that Pentheus' reason be darkened so he will dress as a woman-in the Dionysian garb he so despised-laughed at in the streets, detected in the ceremony, and killed.

Comment

Pentheus decision to dress as a woman is intended to be taken as an indication of his moral debasement.

Third Stasimon (862-911)

The Chorus sing of peace and of the eternal love beauty inspires. Those who fail to understand this and who strive in pride beyond their limits are ruthlessly punished. Those who know that merely to live is happiness are in heaven.

Comment

This scene is one of the most awesome in all Greek tragedy. Dionysus, still disguised as a human, has taken command of the situation, while pretending to cater to Pentheus' desires. This command appears in two forms: (1) dramatically, Dionysus as the Stranger is obviously guiding Pentheus' actions; and (2) thematically, Pentheus is acting the way he is because the spirit of Dionysus has entered into him.

Fourth Episode (912-976)

Pentheus comes out dressed as a woman. He is in a strangely exalted state, seeing everything double. Dionysus appears to him to have taken on a bull's form. With Dionysus helping him, he arranges his dress and worries about his hair with finicky care. In one moment he asks to know the correct way to hold the thyrsus, in the next he considers lifting Mount Cithaeron onto his shoulders. Seeming to have forgotten his original purpose, he becomes all giddy in the thought of his mother heading back to town in triumph.

Comment

It is natural that Pentheus see Dionysus in the form of a bull, for earlier (ll. 618-19), Pentheus attacked a bull, thinking it was Dionysus; furthermore, Dionysus was often worshipped in a bull's form. (Plutarch tells us of an ancient hymn to Dionysus with the following line: "With ox's feet you rage, worthy Bull.")

Fourth Stasimon (977-1023)

The Chorus is an ode contrasting sharply in tone with the previous one, vengefully look forward to the discovery and punishment of Pentheus. Knowledge, they say, is good to seek, but the world also has a spirit of mystery which is not to be denied.

Comment

Like odes in many other Greek plays, this one is imagined to take place over a long period of time, so that all the messenger will describe has had time to take place.

Fifth Episode (1024-1152)

A messenger rushes in with the news that King Pentheus is dead. He had been with the group which went to the mountain, where they hid to watch the women. Pentheus wanted a better view, so Dionysus bent a tall pine tree over, and it carried the king to where he could see, and be seen. Dionysus called the women and they tried to stone him, but he was too high. Then they all gripped the tree and tore it down. Agave stood over her son; he removed his headdress and begged for mercy. She, wrapt in a Dionysian frenzy, did not recognize him, and, with her foot on his side, tugged at his arm and pulled it off, His aunt, Ino, pulled off his other arm, and soon women were running around with various pieces of his body. Agave put his head on the end of her thyrsus and is now bearing it toward the city.

Fifth Stasimon And Exodos (1153-1392)

The Chorus sing of the triumph over Pentheus, but when Agave comes in they are horrified to see her carrying Pentheus' head. Agave thinks she is carrying the head of a lion, and shouts for Cadmus and Pentheus to come out and see what the women have caught with their own hands. Cadmus comes from the mountain, with men carrying the pieces of Pentheus' body. Agave brags to him of her trophy and shows him the head. Cadmus tries to bring her back to her senses; she slowly comes out of the frenzy with no knowledge of the events which have occurred since Dionysus put the spell on all the women of Thebes.

Cadmus laments over the body of Pentheus, praising him as a just man, quick to attack dishonor. (Between lines 1329 and 1330 about fifty lines have been lost from Euripides' original text. But, as authors as late as the twelfth century A.D. quoted and adapted lines from this section, it is possible to present, as William Arrowsmith does in his translation, a fairly clear idea of what has dropped out.)

Dionysus appears as a **deus ex machina** and (where the manuscript takes up again) tells Cadmus of his future wanderings as punishment for not accepting Dionysus. He and Agave acknowledge their sin and beg forgiveness, but Dionysus remains adamant.

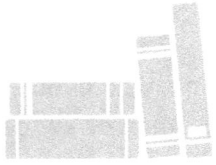

THE PLAYS OF EURIPIDES

IPHIGENIA IN AULIS

BACKGROUND

Iphigenia in Aulis was written near the end of Euripides' life and left unfinished. It is generally believed that the final scene was written by Euripides' son.

After Paris took Helen to Troy, Helen's husband, Menelaus, appealed to his powerful brother, Agamemnon, for help in getting her back. Agamemnon assembled the Greek leaders and their men at the port of Aulis. When their sailing was delayed by unfavorable winds, the prophet Calchas said that Agamemnon had offended the goddess Artemis and must sacrifice his daughter.

CHARACTERS

Agamemnon: King of Argos, leader of the Greek army.

Clytemnestra: Agamemnon's wife

Menelaus: Brother of Agamemnon and husband of Helen.

Iphigenia: Agamemnon's daughter.

Orestes: Agamemnon's small son.

Achilles: Leader of a group of soldiers known as the Myrmidons.

Chorus: Women from Chalcis.

Servant

Messenger

SETTING

The camp of the Greek army at Aulis, a port about forty miles north of Athens, on the Euboean Gulf.

Agamemnon calls his old servant out of his tent to take a letter written during the night to Clytemnestra. He tells the servant that asking Clytemnestra to bring Iphigenia to marry Achilles was a trick-she was to have been sacrificed to Artemis. He has changed his mind, and now countermands the request.

Comment

In this prologue there is a passage of about forty lines that many scholars consider to be spurious. In it Agamemnon tells the story of Helen. Other parts of the text have also been questioned;

some editors believe that a production copy, with changes, has survived rather than Euripides' original version.

The Chorus of women say that they have come from Chalcis, across the Euboean Gulf, to see the spectacle of the great army. (In a disputed passage, they describe the Greek heroes and the ships.)

The servant of Agamemnon has been intercepted by Menelaus and they fight over the letter; Menelaus wants to show it to the army. Agamemnon hears the uproar and comes out. Menelaus accuses him of being changeable and weak. Every man's friend when he wanted to lead the expedition, he had voluntarily sent for Iphigenia: now he has betrayed the Greek cause. Agamemnon replies that Menelaus, unable to hold his wife, should not expect him to sacrifice a daughter for a runaway wife. He says Menelaus has gone mad and sent Greece mad too. The quarrel is interrupted by a messenger who announces that Clytemnestra has arrived with Iphigenia and Orestes for the wedding. Agamemnon bewails the fact that a king must often serve the mob: the army will surely demand the sacrifice. How, meanwhile, can he face Clytemnestra? At the sight of his suffering, Menelaus repents of wanting the war and the sacrifice. But Agamemnon believes the situation to be out of hand, now that Iphigenia has arrived. Both the prophet Calchas and Odysseus know that Agamemnon is generally believed to have offended Artemis, and that the goddess requires propitiation. They are ambitious men and would arouse the army. He asks Menelaus and the Chorus to help keep the truth from Clytemnestra until the sacrifice has been made.

Comment

Some critics find the vacillation of both Agamemnon and Menelaus in this scene an abandonment of character portrayal for the sake of melodramatic excitement. Other critics regard it as realistic character portrayal.

The Chorus sing that passionate love is dangerous, and pray that it never comes to them. From the love of Paris and Helen has come a war.

The arrival of Clytemnestra, Iphigenia, and the baby Orestes has caused great excitement, which the Chorus reflect as they help them down from the chariot. Iphigenia runs to her father with greetings, but is puzzled by his sadness. After Iphigenia has gone inside, Clytemnestra inquires about Achilles' family. Agamemnon tries to get her to return home immediately and look after their other daughters while he takes care of the wedding.

The Chorus sing of Troy, cheerfully assuming that the Greeks will win and Helen will be punished.

Achilles comes looking for Agamemnon; his soldiers are impatient to sail against Troy or go home. Clytemnestra greets him and learns that he has no plans for marrying Iphigenia. The servant tells them that the marriage was a trick of Agamemnon's to get Iphigenia there for the sacrifice. Now that she is in the camp, Clytemnestra is helpless and begs Achilles for help. Outraged that his name should have been used, Achilles promises to prevent the sacrifice. Achilles suggests that she try to argue Agamemnon into changing his mind. She says that Agamemnon is a coward and afraid of the army. He urges her to try anyway, promising to act if Agamemnon insists on sacrificing Iphigenia.

The Chorus sing of the marriage of Achilles' parents. They contrast this to the death awaiting Iphigenia.

Agamemnon announces that the sacrifice, usual before weddings, is prepared. Clytemnestra summons Iphigenia and Orestes and accuses Agamemnon of deceit. In her fury she tells him that she never loved him. She asks what kind of welcome she can give him in Argos after brooding alone over the death of Iphigenia while he fights. She demands to know why lots were not drawn if a sacrifice had to be made. Iphigenia, too, begs for her own life, reminding him of happy times spent together in the past, and she has little Orestes kneel before his father. Agamemnon justifies himself by pleading national necessity. He claims that no Greek wife will be safe from Trojan marauders if the war to avenge Helen's abduction is not fought out. Achilles enters with the news that the army is demanding the sacrifice. He was stoned when he tried to save her-even his own men turned against him. Under the leadership of Odysseus, the men are coming to claim Iphigenia. Achilles swears to defend her against the entire army.

Suddenly Iphigenia announces that she will submit to being sacrificed. All Greece needs her, she says, and she cannot let Achilles die defending a woman. Achilles admires this offer so much he wants to marry her and promises to be near the altar in case she changes her mind at the last minute. Iphigenia says farewell to her mother, urging her not to hate Agamemnon. Clytemnestra faints, and Iphigenia bids the Chorus sing a hymn to Artemis.

(The conclusion is usually attributed to Euripides' son.) A messenger describes to Clytemnestra the sacrifice. When the priest raised his knife, Iphigenia disappeared and a deer lay in her place. Calchas has said the goddess Artemis made the substitution because of Iphigenia's generosity. Clytemnestra refuses to believe the story of the substitution, saying that they are trying to cheat her even of her sorrow. (A surviving fragment indicates that the play may originally have ended with Artemis appearing as a **deus ex machina** and consoling Clytemnestra.)

Comment

This play contains the best statement of Clytemnestra's case against Agamemnon. His usually heroic stature is reduced by his vacillation, and the generosity of Iphigenia makes a sharp contrast to the selfishness of Helen.

THE PLAYS OF EURIPIDES

RHESUS

BACKGROUND

For a long time this play was considered spurious by Classical scholars since it seems to unlike other plays of Euripides. In antiquity, however, except for one anonymous note, the play was accepted as a genuine work of Euripides. William Ritchie, in a recent long and close study of the play's authenticity, shows almost beyond doubt that Euripides wrote it and that what had most disturbed scholars can be attributed to the fact that it is an early work of the playwright. The play is based on the tenth book of the *Iliad* but has two important changes. It presents the Trojan point of view (unsympathetically) instead of the Greek; Athena twice intervenes and gives information which affects the action-something which occurs in no other Greek tragedy.

In the *Iliad*, the action just before the tenth book show the Greeks on the defensive. They have built a wall and a ditch to assist in the defense of their ships. The Trojans are camped outside the ditch, waiting to attack.

THE PLAYS OF EURIPIDES

CHARACTERS

Hector: Son of King Priam of Troy and the leader of the Trojan army.

Paris: Also called Alexander, brother of Hector.

Aeneas: A Trojan prince.

Dolon: A Trojan warrior.

Rhesus: King of Thrace, a country north of Troy.

Athracian: Driver of King Rhesus' chariot.

Odysseus: A Greek leader, famous for being crafty.

Diomedes: Greek leader famous for bravery.

Athena: Goddess who favors the Greeks to win.

Muse Of The Mountains: Divine figure, mother of Rhesus.

Shepherd

Chorus: Trojan guards.

SETTING

In front of the tent of Hector, on a plain outside the walls of Troy.

The Trojan guards come in from their outposts in great turmoil, shouting for Hector. They have seen many fires and large movements of men behind the Greek lines. Hector believes it means the Greeks are planning to withdraw. He wants to summon the army and attack when they try to board the ships, but Aeneas enters and warns him that the activity may have some other meaning. He suggests they send a spy to discover what is actually happening. Dolon volunteers, asking that for his reward he receive the immortal horses of Achilles when the Greeks are defeated. He will disguise himself as a wolf. Pausing to look toward the Greek camp, he thinks of what glory might be his if he could kill Odysseus or even Diomedes.

Comment

There is considerable use of dramatic **irony** (see General Introduction) in this scene. Knowing that the Greeks will triumph, the audience can see the Trojan boasting for what it is. The use of **irony** perhaps becomes excessive when Dolon chooses the two heroes he will be killed by as those he would like himself to kill.

The Chorus pray to Apollo that Dolon's mission will be successful.

A shepherd who has left his flock on nearby Mount Ida enters with the news that King Rhesus is approaching with his army. Hector proudly states that the Trojans do not need Rhesus now that they are winning. Where was he when they were losing? The wiser counsel of the Chorus persuades him to accept the offered help, however. The Chorus sing a joyful ode of welcome to Rhesus, who enters in great state. Hector frankly tells him he should have come sooner. Rhesus explains that he started for Troy once before, but that his neighbors to the north, the Scythians, had invaded his country. As soon as they were defeated, he started for Troy. He and his troops are war-hardened now, and he promises to defeat the Greeks, capture their princes, and burn their ships within a day. The Trojan soldiers cheer him and he promises to join Hector in an expedition to attack Greece.

Not wanting to take honor away from Hector by defeating the Greeks by himself, Rhesus offers to restrict his effort to fighting Achilles. Hector tells him this is impossible because Achilles has refused to fight, being angry with Agamemnon. Hector suggests that Rhesus face the forces of Odysseus, the Greek leader who stole Athena's image from her sanctuary in Troy, and who successfully spied on Troy disguised as a priest. Rhesus promises to face him and punish him like a thief. Hector says nothing can be done until Dolon returns; he takes Rhesus to a camp site.

The guards are still frightened by the activity in the Greek camp and, as soon as their watch is up, go out to seek the relief guards.

Odysseus and Diomedes, Greek leaders reconnoitering in the Trojan camp, enter cautiously. On his belt, Diomedes has Dolon's wolfskin and mask. Drawing their swords, they rush into Hector's tent. From what they say, it becomes evident that before killing him they learned from Dolon the layout of the camp. Disappointed in this murderous search for Hector, they decide to return to their own lines. Suddenly Athena appears and tells them that the important person for them to kill is Rhesus, for if he lives till morning, the Greeks will lose the war. She tells them where he is sleeping and that near him are his famous white horses. She warns them that Paris is approaching

Hector's tent. They want to kill him, but she says it has been ordained that someone else do that. They go out to seek Rhesus, and, when Paris enters in search of Hector, Athena appears in the form of Aphrodite, his favorite divinity. She speaks softly to him and quiets his alarm over the reports he has heard of spies in the camp. When he leaves, she shouts to warn Odysseus and Diomedes that the dead body of Rhesus has been discovered. They are pursued and caught, but after giving the password Dolon told them, they are released. Odysseus says he saw the killers running off, and the soldiers go in pursuit.

The Chorus now believe Odysseus has been in the camp; they are frightened that Hector will punish them for letting him by.

Wounded, the charioteer of Rhesus staggers in and tells how Rhesus was killed in his sleep and the horses stolen. Hector storms in and tells the Captain of the Guard he'll be executed for his negligence. The Charioteer accuses Hector of killing the king to get the horses. Hector patiently denies the charge; he believes that only Odysseus could have gotten through the lines so quietly.

The Muse of the Mountains, mother of King Rhesus, appears, holding the dead body of her son in her arms. She laments the death of her son and curses Odysseus, Diomedes, and Helen. She tells of the shame she felt after having a child by the River Strymon, and of how the sea maidens raised Rhesus; of how she tried to keep him from coming to Troy; and how Athena was the cause of his death. She predicts the death of Achilles. Hector goes out to rouse his men for the day's battle.

THE PLAYS OF EURIPIDES

CRITICISM

CONTEMPORARY

As with all knowledge of antiquity, our knowledge of contemporary critical opinion of Euripides' work must be for the most part inferred. The extent of this loss may be suggested by recalling that of the more than 90 plays written by Euripides (of which the names of 81 are known) only 19 have survived; however, drama that functions as part of a formally acknowledged religious festival is less apt to receive the kind of criticism we think of as dramatic criticism than secular theater. It must also be remembered that Euripides began to write at a time, shortly after Aeschylus' death, when competition in festivals was extremely great. Not only was Sophocles, already established for ten years as a major playwright, to write for 50 more years, but to other, now-forgotten dramatists went at least half of the victories. These considerations, added to the novelty of his plays, make understandable the fact that Euripides won first prize only five times in 50 years. Yet it is a measure of Euripides' achievement that his popularity grew enormously after his death-so much so that he out-ranked the other two masters of Greek drama.

Athenian mourning for Euripides' death was, we know, led by the example of Sophocles; and his Macedonian plays received four first prizes posthumously, despite the attack of Aristophanes in the *Frogs* a few months before. Besides Sophocles, Socrates and, perhaps, Thucydides, may be counted as acknowledging to some extent the merits of Euripides. Sophocles formally criticized Euripides' **realism**, but he imitated the prologue form of Euripides in his own *Women of Trachis* and the **deus ex machina** in the *Philoctetes*. Socrates is reported to have attended only Euripides' tragedies and never those by any other dramatist. Thucydides may have been the author of the memorial praise inscribed on the cenotaph at Athens.

LATER ANTIQUITY

But it is fourth century (B.C.) Greece which acclaims Euripides, both directly and indirectly, Aristotle praises the dignity in simplicity achieved by Euripides, as does the author of Treatise on the Sublime. It is the Euripidean rhetoric which they honor. The indirect commentary is seen in the influence of Euripides, not only in the tragedies of this age but in Menander's New Comedy. The same rhetorical skill has endeared Euripides' work to critics in many ages. Terence, in his Palatine Anthology, remarks the difficulty of achieving the simple dignity of Euripides.

MODERN CRITICISM

The generalization which says that Euripides has largely been the discovery of poets and the nemesis of critics is not altogether unfounded. In England, Shelley not only translated some of euripides' work, but himself achieved something of the same style, especially in the Cenci. In France, Racine was responsible for a great rejuvenation of Euripides by adapting many of the plays. Later, in the nineteenth century, a number of French scholars contributed to Euripidean criticism, often in comparison with the French Classical Drama. And in Germany, Nietzsche celebrated Euripides as a master in the attainment of that direct simplicity which he noted generally as a Greek trait: "Die Griechen Sind, wie das Genie, einfach: des halb sind sie die unsferer Lehrer [The Greeks are, like Genius, simple: therefore they are the immortal teachers]."

THE CRITICAL CRUX

One point has been the major center of critical attention-the apparent disparity between the complete integration of the gods into the fabric of the plays and Euripides' actual beliefs. The considerations of this problem has led in two distinct directions-the rationalists would suggest that Euripides had a conscious interest in trying to effect a social reform; whereas the symbolist or romantic critics formulate an intent of stylistic motive culminating in an entirely organized system of symbols. The former is the position of Verrall and the other rationalists, especially Gilbert Murray. The contrasting view is more akin to that of Shelley and Nietzsche. A moderator of note between these two extremes is Professor Kitto. Much of the current popularity of Euripidean drama is dependent upon the work of Professors Murray and Kitto, although the former has been criticized at times for being overly romantic in his approach (especially in his translations, which are, however, excellent verse).

THE PLAYS OF EURIPIDES

ESSAY QUESTIONS AND ANSWERS

Question: What are the characteristic features of Euripides' plays?

Answer: Formal structure: long, expository prologues; formal, line-by-line conversations; evenly balanced argumentative speeches; deus ex machina in conclusions. Radical content: realistic characters; attacks on women (and enthusiastic feminism).

Question: In what respects is *Alcestis* not a tragedy?

Answer: The most important nontragic feature of *Alcestis* is its happy ending. Also, the presence of Heracles and his drunken behavior are comic. Lastly, the characters of Admetus and his father, Pheres, are presented realistically-a feature not found much in early tragedy.

Question: How does Euripides gain sympathy for Medea?

Answer: By showing that she is loved by her Nurse and by the women of Corinth; by showing Jason to be despicable; by showing her inner struggle before she kills her children.

Question: What does *Medea* show about Euripides' attitude toward women?

Answer: Often accused of misogyny, and partly because he represented in this play a woman who killed her own children, Euripides could defend himself by pointing to the many feminist arguments in *Medea.* Medea says that women suffer at the hands of men and that she is not going to be a victim of this situation. The Chorus not only agree with her, but amplify the position.

Question: How is the scene with Aegeus relevant to Medea?

Answer: The lament of Aegeus for his childlessness shows how Jason will feel when his children are dead. Aegeus gives a refuge to Medea, who is completely cut off from any help her family might have given her. The scene's ode to Athens gives an opportunity for the arguments against Medea's plan to be stated.

Question: What is unusual about the structure of *Hippolytus?*

Answer: The goddess Aphrodite appears in the Prologue and tells in great detail what will happen. This is apparently done to free Phaedra from ultimate responsibility for her love. An earlier version by Euripides had been severely criticized because her love was a crime.

Question: What is the symbolism in *Hippolytus?*

Answer: The mortals Phaedra and Hippolytus are symbols of the conflicting natural forces of love and chastity. On the divine level these forces are represented by Aphrodite and Artemis.

Question: How is the symbolical conflict in *Hippolytus* resolved?

Answer: By an appeal to the "golden mean": the avoidance of either extreme of love or chastity.

Question: What features make *Hippolytus* characteristically Euripidean?

Answer: Expository prologue: interest in abnormal psychology; comedy and **realism** in the Nurse; use of **deus ex machina**; formal, balanced argumentative speeches.

Question: Why are *The Heracleidae* and *Andromache* called "political plays"?

Answer: Like other plays of Euripides, these two plays glorify Athens at the time she was at war with Sparta. *The Heracleidae* gives historical reasons intended to show that the two cities should be friendly. *Andromache* attacks the character of Spartans in Menelaus and Hermione, and the god who sided with Sparta, Apollo.

Question: Why is *Hecuba,* like some other plays by Euripides, called a melodrama?

Answer: The play has a happy ending, which places it outside the **genre** of pure tragedy. As is characteristic of melodrama, the action of this play is sensational and violent, and the emotion evoked by the action is intense pathos.

Question: What is a satyr-play?

Answer: A satyr-play is the name given to the fourth play of a tetralogy presented in the Dionysian festivals. It was required to be light in tone, and formed a contrast to the three preceding tragedies. The Chorus consisted of a group of Satyrs given to drinking, wenching, and coarse humor. Euripides' *Cyclops* is the only satyrplay to have survived.

Question: In what way is the form of *Heracles* typical of Euripides?

Answer: The play falls into two parts which are only loosely related to one another. In the first part Heracles is raised to the heights of triumph when he kills Lycus, who had tried to kill Heracles' wife and children. In the second part he goes mad, kills his wife and children himself, and is thrown to the depths of despair. There is no necessary connection between the two actions.

Question: What is Euripides' attitude to the gods in *Heracles*?

Answer: When Heracles denies that gods commit evil acts, we see a typical Euripidean effort to make the gods rational, ideal beings.

Question: What are the **themes** of *The Suppliants?*

Answer: The play is fundamentally a glorification of Athens for its democracy, its hospitality to the oppressed, and its rational attitudes. War and the lack of reason in political leaders are condemned.

Question: What are the melodramatic elements of *Ion*?

Answer: A romantic **theme** of intrigue and love between mortals and men; exciting coincidences; the recognition of an orphan by his true parents through tokens; happy ending.

Question: What is the attitude toward the gods in Ion?

Answer: This play expresses the typical Euripidean skepticism towards the traditional stories of the gods. Apollo is shown to be irresponsible in his behavior toward Creusa; it is confirmed when he does not appear at the end lest he be embarrassed.

Question: In what way is the meaning of *Iphigenia in Tauris* comparable to the sacrifice of Isaac in the Old Testament?

Answer: Both stories reflect an earlier age in which human beings were sacrificed to the gods. When animals are substituted by divine intervention, the later practice of sacrificing animals is instituted. Since both explain the origin of customs, they are called "etiological" stories. In both stories the sacrifice of a human was originally a test of faith. (In *Iphigenia in Tauris*, of course, the test of faith is only implied by recalling Agamemnon's situation.)

Question: What is the **theme** of *The Trojan Women?*

Answer: The play is a powerful denunciation of war. It argues that both the defeated and the victors suffer far more than they gain.

Question: What causes the suffering of the triumphant Greeks in *The Trojan Women?*

Answer: In the play itself, of course, the Greeks do not suffer; they are a triumphant army dividing the spoils. The nature of their future suffering is foretold by Cassandra; the cause is seen in the play. The Greeks sin by committing a number of acts of hubris: the murder of King Priam at the altar where he sought sanctuary; the attempt to rape Cassandra at the altar; the sacrifice of Polyxena. This is the reason Athena turns against the Greeks after the war. Flushed with triumph, the Greeks vaunted themselves too highly.

Question: What gives unity to the structure of *The Trojan Women?*

Answer: Usually described as episodic, the scenes in the play are given some unity by the constant presence of Hecuba on stage, and by the fact that each **episode** is related to the **themes** of Trojan suffering and Greek sin.

Question: What is the attitude of Euripides toward Helen in *The Trojan Women?*

Answer: To Helen's traditional fame as the most beautiful woman in the world, Euripides adds a character that is proud, vain, and selfish. She is shown as being without remorse for the suffering she caused as a result of her illicit love for Paris. Her only desire is to protect herself; at no time does she express sympathy for or any desire to help the Trojan women with whom she lived for ten years. Her affections are shown to be changeable. She lies whenever it will serve her purpose.

Question: How does Euripides intensify Electra's suffering in *Electra?*

Answer: Euripides changes the traditional story of Electra by showing her as married to a peasant. He contrasts her poverty with the regal splendor of her mother, Clytemnestra.

Question: Why was Electra's marriage to the peasant never consummated?

Answer: Her marriage to the peasant was never consummated because he realized she was forced to marry him and had too much respect for her to do anything against her wishes.

Question: How does Euripides criticize Aeschylus' version of *Electra?*

Answer: He is particularly distressed by what he considered to be the unlikely coincidences of the clues Aeschylus used in the recognition scene between Electra and Orestes. Euripides also treats the order of Apollo to kill Clytemnestra with more skepticism. He condemns the sin of Orestes more strongly.

Question: Describe the character of Orestes.

Answer: Orestes is vacillating and relatively weak. He is extremely cautious, not revealing his identity until the old servant recognizes him. He is reluctant to kill his mother at the last minute and has to be encouraged by his sister, Electra. This representation of Orestes gives credence to his remorse, which follows as soon as the murder is committed.

Question: How is Euripides' Clytemnestra different from that of Aeschylus?

Answer: In Euripides, Clytemnestra is shown to be remorseful for the murder of her husband, Agamemnon. She is the victim of her love for Aegisthus, rather than a towering monument of hate. She tries to help Electra and protect her against Aegisthus. She is reasonable and conciliatory when she meets Electra.

Question: In what way is *Helen* not typical of Euripides?

Answer: In this play, Helen is treated sympathetically; usually Euripides attacks her violently for having been responsible for the Trojan War. By following the version of Helen's life in which a phantom goes off with Paris, the real Helen is absolved of responsibility.

Question: In what ways is *Helen* characteristic of Euripides' later plays?

Answer: The play is a melodrama, with such romantic elements as an exotic foreign setting and an exciting escape. In plot, the play is almost identical to *Iphigenia in Tauris*, almost as if the later play were an imitation of the earlier one. Also, the Chorus has little involvement with the action, and historically, the Chorus developed toward the status of an interlude.

Question: Why does *Phoenissae* have the title it does?

Answer: It was a **convention** to name Greek plays for their Choruses when the play had no very strong **protagonist**. Usually, as in *The Trojan Women*, the Chorus is, in a sense, the **protagonist**. In *Phoenissae,* however, the Chorus of Phoenician women just happen to be in Thebes on their way through the city.

Question: What changes does Euripides make in the usual story of Laius' family in *Phoenissae?*

Answer: In the usual version, Jocasta kills herself as soon as she learns she had unknowingly married her son, Oedipus. Here she does not commit suicide until after the death of her sons by Oedipus-Eteocles and Polyneices. Also, Oedipus is still living in

Thebes; in the usual version he exiles himself when he discovers he has married his mother.

Question: What is the political **theme** of *Phoenissae?*

Answer: The play criticizes ambition and lust for power. The qualities are represented by Eteocles. More desirable qualities are represented in his brother, Polyneices, who considers virtue to be the end of life. The character of Menoeceus represents an individual who is willing to die for the good of the state. In this respect, he is a purer example of patriotism than Polyneices because he has no personal reward at stake.

Question: What characteristics of Euripidean drama are found in *Orestes?*

Answer: Interest in abnormal behavior: here the madness of Orestes; melodramatic action: here the attempts to kill Helen and Hermoine and the burning of the palace: the formal debate: here between Tyndareus and Orestes; comic **realism**: here in the figure of the Phrygian Eunuch.

Question: In what ways is the *Bacchae* not typical of late Euripidean tragedy?

Answer: The play reverts to an older, "Aeschylean' 'type of structure with its prominent, well-integrated Chorus, its long choral passages, its interest in religious morality, and its condemnation of hubris.

Question: What is the **theme** of the *Bacchae?*

Answer: The central **theme** is that of man's relationship to the gods; Pentheus sins when he refuses to believe in Dionysus.

Associated with this is the **theme** of instinctive behavior and its merits. Interest in physical pleasure is natural: It is expected by the gods.

Excessive abandonment of the self to physical pleasure makes the individual a brute (e.g., Agave's killing of Pentheus). The natural world contains both beauty and danger.

Question: What does Dionysus represent?

Answer: Dionysus is god of fertility and of wine. By extension, he is a symbol of natural appetites, pleasure, and emotion.

Question: Describe the character of Pentheus.

Answer: King Pentheus is basically a well-intentioned boy, but he lacks imagination. He is inflexible and opposed to change. He apparently refuses to trust his own emotions and cannot adapt to circumstances. In the case of the miracles, he refused to believe the evidence of his own eyes. He is dedicated to the philosophy of rationalism until it becomes a vice. Under his moral exterior, he is prurient.

Question: Why is *Iphigenia in Aulis* called realistic?

Answer: The actions of the characters are well motivated, natural, and credible. Such traditionally heroic figures as Agamemnon and Clytemnestra are represented in a "domestic" situation with all the doubts, fears, and weaknesses of ordinary mortals.

Question: What is the historical significance of the **realism** in *Iphigenia in Aulis*?

Answer: The play shows Greek drama in transition to Middle and New Comedy, in which ordinary people were shown in domestic situations.

Question: What is the source of *Rhesus?*

Answer: Book X of the *Iliad*. It changes the story of the original by presenting the Trojan point of view and by presenting Athena as intervening directly in the affairs of humans.

Question: Describe the character of Odysseus.

Answer: Odysseus is traditionally described as "wily." His fame for trickery is so great that when a spy is suspected in *Rhesus,* Odysseus is immediately thought of.

BIBLIOGRAPHY

Much of our knowledge of Euripides depends on the tremendous surge of philological scholarship in nineteenth-century Germany and on the wealth of dramatic studies in France of the same era. Recently, studies of classical philology in English have applied modern linguistic methods to the study of Euripides. Of the first two groups, the major works have been included in this bibliography; of the last, a few representative studies are listed- in none of these three areas should the present bibliography be considered exhaustive. The remainder of the works included are more recent attempts to bring Euripides or the Greek culture before the English reading public. The works have been listed alphabetically and a key has been included, given below, to aid the student in treating any particular area. If, for example, the problem under consideration is Euripides' influence on other dramatists, the student should locate all works with the code A2c. Annotation is included for most of the works.

KEY

(A) Euripides

(1) Translations

(a) Plays (b) Fragments (c) Lost Plays

(2) Criticism

(a) Plays (b) Specific Texts (c) Relation to other dramatists or theaters.

(3) Biography

(B) Background

(1) Dramatic (2) Socio-Historical

(C) Reference

B2

Agard, W. R., *The Greek Mind,* Princeton Univ. Press, 1957.

C

Allen, James T., *A Concordance to Euripides*, Berkeley, Univ. of Calif. Press, 1954.

A2a

Anthon, Charles, *An English Commentary on the Rhesus, Medea, Hippolytus, Alcestis, Heracleidae, Supplices, and Troades of Euripides*, with the scanning of each play from the latest and best authorities, New York, Harper, 1877. Difficult to obtain, but extremely useful.

A2a

Appleton, Reginald B., *Euripides the Idealist*, New York, Dutton, 1927. Searches for the secondary meaning behind the obvious in Euripides. A reaction to Verrall and the rationalists and realists.

A1b

Arnim, H. von, ed., *Supplemendum Euripideum*, Bonn, 1912. Presents the papyri discovered from Nauck (below) to date of writing. Has been criticized by Murray for metrical errors.

A2a A2b

Bates, William N., *Euripides: a Student of Human Nature*, New York, Dutton, 1927. Treats Euripides as primarily an observer of man and his predicament; a variation of the realist view. Includes a chapter on "Euripides in the papyri," pp. 305-8.

A2a

Blaklock, E. M., *The Male Characters of Euripides: a study in **realism***, Wellington, New Zealand, Univ. Press, 1952. A modern realist treatment.

B2

Bowra, C. M., *The Greek Experience,* New York, 1958. General, popular treatment.

A2b

Burnett, S. P., "Virtues of Admetus," *Classical Philology*, LX, October, 1965 (pp. 240-55). A new look at the character of Admetus in the *Alcestis* from the standpoint of his ethical situation.

C B2

Cambridge Ancient History, Vol. V, Cambridge, 1935.

A1a

The Complete Greek Drama, ed., Whitney J. Oates and Eugene O'Neill, Jr., 2 vols., New York, Random, 1938. Various translators. Euripides is at the end of Vol. I and beginning of Vol. II. For a comparative study of the Greek playwrights, this offers the handiest compilation of texts.

A1a

The Complete Greek Tragedies, Vol. 3-4, Chicago, Univ. of Chicago Press, 1955; 1959. Introduction by Richmond Lattimore; translations by R. Lattimore, R. Warner, R. Gladstone, D. Grene, W. Arrowsmith, W. Brynner.

A2b

Davidson, J. A., "Euripides' Media 1181-4," *Classical Review*, New Series, XIV, December 1964 (pp. 240-1).

A2

Decharme, Paul, *Euripide et L'esprit de son theatre*, Paris, 1893. Translation, *Euripides and the Spirit of his Dramas*, James Loeb, tr., New York, Macmillan, 1906; 1909. An excellent work. First three chapters give a complete elaboration of the religious and philosophical views of Euripides.

A3

Delcourt, Marie, *La vie d'Euripide*, Paris, Gallimard, 1930.

A2a

Delebecque, Edouard, *Euripide et la guerre du Peloponnese*, Paris, C. Klincksieck, 1951. A detailed study of the relationship of the Peloponnesian War to the attitude of Euripides as expressed in his plays.

A2

Eliot, T. S., "Euripides and Professor Murray," *Selected Essays, 1917-1932*, New York, Harcourt, Brace & World, Inc., 1932 (pp. 46-50). Eliot's view of the effect of Murray's translation and popularization of Euripides.

B1 A2c

Flickinger, R. C., *The Greek Theatre and Its Drama*, Chicago, 1922. A general study.

C

Graves, Robert, *The Greek Myths*, 2 vols. Harmondsworth, Middlesex, England, Penguin, 1955. A popular rendition of the Greek myths which sometimes fails to name the authorities for the various versions of the myths. Extremely useful list of significances of names.

B2

Greene, William Chase, *Moira: Fate, Good, and Evil in Greek Thought*, Harvard Univ. Press, 1944.

A2a

Greenwood, Leonard H. G., *Aspects of Euripidean Tragedy*, Cambridge Univ. Press, 1953. A study based largely on Kitto's work but going beyond Kitto's conclusions, suggesting that Euripides was impeded in his portrayal of real human action by the traditional view of the gods. Scholarly and important. Summarizes earlier critical positions.

A2a

Grube, Georges M. A., *The Drama of Euripides*, London, Methuen, 1941. An energetic symbolist interpretation.

B2

Hamilton, Edith, *The Greek Way to Western Civilization*, New York, 1948. A popularization of Greek culture.

C

Harsh, Philip W., *A Handbook of Classical Drama*, Stanford, Univ. Press. 1960.

C

Harvey, Sir Paul, *The Oxford Companion to Classical Literature*, Oxford, Univ. Press. 1937.

A2c

Heinemann, Karl, *Die Tragischen Gestalten der Griechen in der Weltliteratur*, in the series *Das Erbe der Alten,* 2 vols., Leipzig, 1920. An illuminating study strictly limited to drama.

A2c

Hettick, Ernest L., A *Study in Ancient Naturalism, the testimony of Euripides*, Williamsport, Pa., Bayard, 1933.

B2 B1

Kitto, H. D. F., *The Greeks, Hamondsworth*, Middlesex, England, Penguin, 1958. A good modern simplified presentation.

B1

Kitto, H. D. F., *Greek Tragedy, a Literary Study*, New York, Doubleday (Anchor), 1954. A good complement to Kitto's other study above.

A2a A2b

Klotsche, Ernest H., "The Supernatural in Euripides as illustrated in prayer, curses, oathes, oracles, prophesies, dreams, and visions," Lincoln, Neb., *Nebraska Univ. Studies*, XVIII, 1918, No. 3-4.

A2b

Lattimore, Richmond, tr., "Fall of the City: three songs from Euripides," *Antioch Review*, XXV, Spring, 1965 (pp. 90-2).

B1

Legrand, P. E., *The New Greek Comedy*, London, 1917. A general study of the rise of the Greek theater, culminating with Menander.

A2c A2a

Lucas, Frank L., *Euripides and his Influence*, Boston, Marshall Jones, 1923; New York, Cooper Sq., 1963. An important study tracing the influence of Euripides from contemporary times to the present. Introduction by R. Lattimore.

A2b A2a

Manning, Clarence A., *A Study of Archaism in Euripides*, New York, Columbia Univ. Press, 1916. (Col. Univ. Studies in Classical Philology-publication of Ph.D. thesis.)

A1a

Medea, freely adapted from the *Medea* of Euripides by Robinson Jeffers, New York, Random, 1946; New York, S. French, 1948. An interesting adaptation by an important American poet.

A1a

Murray, Gilbert, tr., *Euripides' plays in 3 vols.* Oxford, 1901-13. Brief critical notes; help in translation from Wilamowitz-Moellendorff and Verrall.

B1

Murray, Gilbert, *The Athenian Drama*, London, 1902. See especially introduction to Vol. II.

A

Murray, Gilbert, *Euripides and his Age*, New York, Holt, 1913; Oxford Univ. Press, 1946. This is perhaps the single most important work for the general reader or beginning student, covering all aspects of Euripidean study.

A1b

Nauck, ed., *Fragmenta Tragicorum Graecorum*, Leipzig, 1889. Still authoritative to the time of publication.

A2a

Nestle, Wilhelm, *Die Philosophische Quellen des Euripides*, Leipzig, 1920. An important critical study historically.

A2c

Nestle, Wilhelm, *Euripides der Dichter der grieschen Aufklarumgm*, Stuttgart, 1901. Useful, though often uncritical.

A2a

Norwood, Gilbert, *Essays on Euripidean Drama*, Berkeley, Univ. of Calif. Press, 1954.

B1 A2c

Norwood, Gilbert, *Greek Comedy*, London, 1932. A good general study.

A2b

Parry, H., "Second Stasimon of Euripides' *Heracles*" (637-700), *American Journal of Philology*, LXXXVI, October, 1965 (pp. 363-74).

A2c A2a

Patin, Henri J. G., *Etudes sur les tregiques grecs* . . . , 3 vols., Paris, Hachette, 1841-3; 1884. Still good, with much comparison of Classical French Tragedy.

A2a

Phoutrides, Aristides E., "The Chorus of Euripides," *Harvard Studies in Classical Philology*, XXVII, Cambridge, 1916 (pp. 77-170).

A1a

The Plays of Euripides in English, ed., Ernest Rhys, 2 vols., New York, Dutton, (Everyman's Library), 1906. Translations by H. H. Milman; Shelley, M. Wodhull, R. Potter.

B1

Prentice, William K., *Those Ancient Dramas Called Tragedies*, Princeton Univ. Press, 1942.

C

Smith's Smaller Classical Dictionary, ed., E. H. Blakeney. Everyman's Library, 1937.

A2b A2c

Turyn, Aleksander, *The Byzantine Ms. tradition of the tragedies of Euripides,* Urbana, Univ. of Illinois Press, Ill. Studies in Language and Literature, Vol. 43, 1957.

A2a

Verrall, A. W., *Euripides, the Rationalist,* Cambridge Univ. Press, 1895. The classical study of Euripides from the standpoint of the realist.

A1a

Way, Arthus S., tr., *Euripides, with an English translation,* 4 vols., New York, Macmillan (The Loeb Classical Library), 1916-19. Has the virtue of all Loeb editions of having a Greek and English text.

A2

Wilamowitz-Moellendorff, Ulrich von, *Analecta Euripidea,* 1875. Hailed by Murray as the foundation of all modern criticism.

A2a A2b

Zuntz, Gunther, *An Inquiry into the transmission of the plays of Euripides,* Cambridge, Univ. Press, 1965.

____, *The Political Plays of Euripides,* Manchester Univ. Press, 1955.